How to Be a

Good Bboy

How to Be a Good Bboy

WHAT A CAT'S KINDNESS TEACHES
US ABOUT HUMAN JUSTICE

Bilbo the Cat
& Ellen Murray

unbound

First published in 2023

Unbound
Level 1, Devonshire House, One Mayfair Place, London W1J 8AJ
www.unbound.com

Text design by PDQ Digital Media Solutions Ltd

A CIP record for this book is available from the British Library

ISBN 978-1-80018-193-9 (hardback)
ISBN 978-1-80018-194-6 (ebook)

Printed in Slovenia by DZS

1 3 5 7 9 8 6 4 2

MIX
Paper | Supporting
responsible forestry
FSC
www.fsc.org
FSC® C106600

For Lyra

Here's to better times ahead, and saying goodbye to bombs and bullets once and for all.

Lyra McKee, 2019

Contents

it is ,now time to ...give kiss

CHAPTER ONE

Hello

Being a cat is easy, or so they say in the papers. I'm lucky enough to have a cat of my own, a bright-orange ginger boy who turned seven years old in August 2021. Bilbo, his name since birth, is fairly large as cats go, and his fur is a delightful mix of vibrant oranges and whites. During his years on this earth, he has amassed over a hundred thousand fans on the internet, raised tens of thousands of pounds for good causes and young artists, been recognised in press and parliaments, and grown a community of caring people who keep up with everything he's up to. Bilbo's my darling boy, and he's a treasure.

Being a human rights activist is also easy, or so they say in the papers. I've been involved in human rights work since 2013, when I was nineteen years old and a naïve university student living alone for the first time. I fell into this particular rabbit hole mostly by chance, and though I have made a meagre wage for most of my career so far, I developed a deep fascination and love for the work, which has helped keep me going to the present day. As I'll explore in the chapters ahead, my start in this work was not typical or secure, nor was it the culmination of years of study or a life goal. My health – and increasing lack of it – have influenced my work greatly, and I've been lucky to learn a lot about myself, human rights and society in general throughout it all. As my colleagues will reliably attest, my screw-ups are at least as numerous as my success stories, and I often feel like I've bullshitted my way into the rooms I get access to. Looking at the hundreds of other activists I've talked to during my career, none of this is unusual, but I want to begin this book by setting expectations. Although in this book I will explore themes that I hope readers find useful, unless I'm talking about my own experiences, nothing I say is authoritative, nor should it be. Although I do advise people – two of my roles until recently were to advise the UK and Northern Ireland governments on LGBTQ topics – I leave it up to the reader to deduce their own paths forward,[1,2] because the type of human rights work that we do individually will always be best informed by our own circumstances, safety and beliefs.

This book is about being a cat, and about being a human rights defender. It's about how you might dip your toe into this sort of work for the first time, and about how the world is changing to bring new dynamics to the work I do, both for the better and for the worse. It's about cynicism, radicalisation, despair and recovery, and it's about the lies we tell ourselves about the work we do. It's about love, joy and kindness, and about how these are all at the core of what Bilbo and I do, with our work together as individuals who try to make folks a little happier and more comforted over the internet. Due to the limitations of science in the 2020s, I will not be covering how to become a cat.

To address the title of this book: 'bboy' means 'boy' in a very particular form of internet cat-speak, developed from decades of online cat culture and adapted for Bilbo. You can pronounce it 'boy', 'buh-boy' or 'bee-boy', whatever makes your heart happiest. My name is Ellen, traditionally a woman's name, so readers may be fairly questioning my knowledge in how to be a good bboy. I have two things on my side which grant me the expertise for a book like this: my co-author is the quintessential model of a good bboy, and I won a trophy emblazoned 'Boy of the Year' in primary school in 2004. I have the qualifications, thank you very much.

im warm ,im safe, im happy

CHAPTER TWO

Ellen the Human

I've lived in Belfast all my life. It's the capital city of Northern Ireland, perched on the northeast coast of the island of Ireland and cradled between Black and Divis Mountains and the Irish Sea. Growing up in the west of the city, I went to an all-boys Catholic primary school which was inexplicably in one half of a school building whose other half was occupied by a completely distinct, legally separate all-girls Catholic primary school. Down the centre of the building was a single corridor, the only shared space in the building, painted the exact shade of blue of the Joint Security Area buildings in Korea's Demilitarised Zone. We got some time off in my third year while the Army dug up an unexploded bomb from the Blitz attack on Belfast during World War II from under the playground, and we sometimes stopped at the chippy on our way back from swimming classes for PE, but otherwise it was pretty normal schooling for a child born in 1990s Belfast. We got some new hopscotch lines out of the bomb scare, and I got my greatest sporting recognition to date from the swimming – my ten-metre badge. In the parlance of the NI peace process, I was a ceasefire baby, being born the year prior to the IRA's 1994 ceasefire, and was in my first year of primary school when the Good Friday Agreement, the Northern Ireland peace agreement, was signed in 1998.

I learned to play the violin both classically and with Irish traditional music through my primary school and the local chapel, and although I enjoyed it, my lack of coordination and unreliable attention put to rest much hope for virtuosity. I preferred singing and enjoyed a prize position as show-off soprano in the front benches of the youth choir at Mass every Sunday. I had a few obsessions – tectonic plates, the asteroid belt between Mars and Jupiter, that sort of thing – but my first true interest was roads. I've never been much into cars, but I built roads out of cardboard, traffic lights out of LEGO, drew pretend streetlights in chalk on the bricks in the backyard of my house, and when the primary school got internet access in 2003, searched for pictures of street signs online. A lot of my interests have changed over the years, but this one has not faded even slightly since then, and roads remain one of my utmost fascinations. It's rewarding having such a strong interest in something you see every day, everywhere you go.

I was the only person from my class to go to the secondary school I ended up in, and although I had few friends for the first several years, I was happy. Thanks to my parents' savvy Christmas present of an electronics kit one year, I quickly developed my second lifelong interest, with the kit leading to both my first electrical burns and my first experiences of accidental mediumwave

AM radio piracy. In art class, an assignment to build a mini art gallery led to my using light-emitting diodes as working lighting, but only in hindsight realising that I'd forgotten to add the resistors needed to stop it catching fire. Luckily, it fizzled out pretty quickly, much like my hopes for a career in art. Wanting to do more, at fifteen I sat my amateur radio licensing exam, meaning I could talk to people all over the world using a simple radio transmitter, bounce voices off the moon and connect to satellites. These little hobbies were useful for getting through a difficult adolescence, where mental health problems and loneliness were regular and skilled players in the game. I struggled with depression for years as a teenager, but interest in electronics and technology got me through the worst, and I continued towards a career in electronics engineering throughout school and university. I had dreams of moving from Northern Ireland to San Francisco and working for Google, hardly a creative goal for an aspiring engineer, but one I thought would lead to fulfilment. Most people wanted to leave Northern Ireland, after all – the 'brain drain', as it was called, and many of my school friends have since left for better lives abroad. Leaving school with just the right number of A-Level qualifications for an engineering course at my local university, I made the first attempt at diving into independent adult life and fell flat on my face. We'll discuss brain bees shortly but to sum up, university was the opposite of what my brain needed to flourish, and I didn't finish my second year. The upside, though, was making friends who changed the direction and meaning of my life, which ultimately led to where I am today, and for the first time I was surrounded by a community I felt a part of.

Gender bomb

Growing up queer in a small, notoriously conservative place like Northern Ireland is always going to have some complications. As a teenager, my school's idea of sex education centred around Catholic teachings, abstinence and blocky JPEG images of what severe cases of sexually transmitted infections look like. We learned about the supposed 40 per cent failure rate of condoms. The horrors of abortion. The taboo of gay affection. My school nailed the shock factor in their delivery, but otherwise it left most of us clueless on the basics of intimate relationships. I was pretty homophobic – not the kind to join Ian Paisley's Save Ulster from Sodomy puritanism but not the kind to extend kindness either. At the same time, I had a growing dreadful knowledge that I was one of those people I despised.

If you had wanted children in the 2000s to become experts in online privacy, the best course of action would have been to break child safeguarding and data protection law and show the evidence to hundreds of witnesses. In 2005, my secondary school did just this, using older prefects – students in senior years appointed to run minor parts of school life – to get access to the younger pupils' social media pages through friend requests, and then showing screenshots at a special assembly. Combining what I learned from this – learn about technology, hide your steps, trust no one – and my growing internal queer shame, I started diving deep into LGBTQ spaces online, which in the mid-2000s were few, but budding. Lurking on various forums for LGBTQ teenagers, and quietly ingesting every queer news story that broke, eventually led to my guard lowering, and I stopped pretending to read forum threads as if I was researching for someone else. I slowly, uncomfortably began to understand who I was.

Something snapped at sixteen years old, and my Catholic faith fell away, veering me briefly into the oncoming lane of irritating early-YouTube atheism. In this era, the platform was chock full of content creators who portrayed themselves as rigidly scientific and unquestionably logical, with a disdain for religious faith and often for the people who held that faith. These online personalities turned many of their fans into annoying and cringeworthy followers with a superiority complex, a persona I embraced wholeheartedly as a fitting contrast to my previous devotion. Time passed, I recovered and jumped onto the new bird on the block, Twitter. I was still deeply in the closet in every way possible, but I had buddies on the computer with their default colourful Twitter eggs for profile pictures.

I joke a lot about how Twitter is an awful website. It is, and it always has been, but it's what connected me to the communities I'm part of today, and it's what springboarded both my work and my dear cat into enough of a spotlight to allow the work I do to be effective. As of August 2021, I've been on the platform for over thirteen years, meaning my Twitter account is now old enough to have a Twitter account, which is a devastating psychic blow every time I think about it. Twitter has seen the rise of social movements for the good and for the bad, and I've met both enemies and lifelong friends on the platform. It's a mixed bag.

Going to university at eighteen years old was scary. I continued to live at home for the first year, moving out for the second to enjoy the new world of rented accommodation, and to see myself be radicalised against landlords. My first student house used pages from tabloid newspapers to support the floor outside the bathroom door, had furnishings clearly pilfered from a recycling yard, and was on the street with the most burglaries in the whole city. It was there that I took some wobbly steps out of the now creaking closet.

Confiding in my university friends, I came out to them as bisexual. Having been unable to be open with others about my sexual orientation until then, I had slowly fallen into a pit of severe depression and anxiety. When you're in the closet, it's hard to tell what life will be like when you open the doors, and the experiences I'd read about told tales of rejection and bullying. I was lucky, and was almost universally shown support and love, and this kindness helped me begin to climb out of the rut I was in. It was quite likely lifesaving, and the experience inspired my interest in human rights work. It didn't seem relevant to tell my family about this fruity arrival, and until the larger of the two queer bombs dropped, they were none the wiser. That second bombshell was gender. Although coming out as bisexual had helped a lot, and had resolved much of the confusion in me, there was a larger issue yet to be addressed. It's hard to describe the experience of growing up and learning that you're transgender without resorting to stereotype and cringe, and, writing this book a decade later, it's still a skill that evades me. From the start of puberty, I had a deep but intangible feeling that I was growing up 'wrongly', that my body wasn't doing what I was expecting or hoping. Researching these feelings online brought up many sad, hopeful stories of people with similar experiences, by those who got happier and those who didn't. At the time, the language transgender people used was much more unstable and changeable than today, and the communities online leaned heavily towards tales of tragedy or were preoccupied with the issue of legitimacy in the eyes of medical science, and most websites featured mermaids, butterflies and other clichés. It still helped, though, and eventually I unearthed small groups of people my own age, with stories that could well have been taken from my own mental journal. Like every telling of trans adolescence, this brushes away more nuance and detail than a landlord's paint job, but it's mostly accurate for my own life.

The next year, in 2013, I told the world I was a transgender woman, and again was beyond lucky to be accepted, including by my family. Immediately coming across clueless doctors and stalling waiting lists, I started my first bit of direct activism – lobbying my local politicians to improve trans healthcare services and improve the waiting lists. This didn't go terribly far, but it was the kickstart I needed to discover that I wanted to do more of it. What I needed most back then was a place to chat with other trans people my age, away from doctors and expectations. This didn't exist in Northern Ireland at the time, and the options for adults back then were too medicalised for comfort, so the microblogging platform Tumblr became the place to search for answers. Eventually it was clear that spaces for people like me did not yet exist, and I moved instead to put out a call for a new group to see if anyone was interested. To my amazement and to the dismay of the owner of the tiny café I unfortunately picked as a location, over a dozen people showed up, and we spent the time just chatting and getting to know each other. It was thrilling, and we agreed to make meetups a regular event, and the numbers slowly grew into what is now a thriving trans youth service that I've long since handed over to people who are still young, GenderJam.

Coming out as trans can be jarring. Depending on how you do so, and especially if and how you transition, you may see the way people treat you change profoundly overnight, and face new challenges walking down the street, finding a public bathroom or going to school. You might be swept into underfunded, outdated mental health services to get access to the healthcare you need, or be told that your first appointment is likely to be in years rather than weeks. Coming out and transitioning are often correctly cited as positive things for trans people's mental health – as they indeed are – but without support, I found myself swapping one basket of problems for another. My mental health was poor before coming out and it was poor after, but the reasons for this changed. Depression caused by being unable to be myself, by hiding secrets, was replaced with anxiety at being laughed at in public, being chased on my bike or being accosted in public facilities. These were rational fears to have – such things happened to the trans friends I'd made, and as it transpired, they happened to me too – but they were clearly not things we intrinsically *had* to experience, they were things we were put through by the society we were in. This now outstandingly obvious idea was the jump-start for what I wanted to do more than anything else – to make things a little bit better.

GenderJam was set up as a charity, led and run by trans young people. It has persisted through a worsening media furore on trans rights and many other struggles along the way, but its principles remain grounded in human rights, self-advocacy and community leadership. I'm proud of that. The motto 'Nothing about us without us' originated within disability rights communities demanding representation in their own campaigns and decisions, and we adopted it as a principle to run the organisation. As a result, when I turned twenty-six, I stood down from the charity so younger trans people could take up the cause, because knowing where you *shouldn't* be is as important as knowing where you *should* be. The issues facing trans young people in the 2020s have changed substantially since 2013, and those living those experiences are best placed to determine how they should be resolved. This new decade has so far seen trans young people and their experiences not only catapulted from relative obscurity in the early 2010s into the media spotlight around the world, but, in many countries, become the target in an emerging, angry culture war against what is still a tiny minority group. Trans young people who came out when I did dealt with the problems of ignorance and niche, but those coming out today deal with the all-encompassing pressure of being a hot political topic, the subject of this year's 'child protection children' crusade.

Since those first experiences, I've accrued more than eight years of knowledge about community organising and human rights work, some of which I'll be laying out in the coming chapters.

im takign a sleep ,please donot disturb

i have juts cleaned . my beans

The bends

I've always been sore. My earliest memory of pain is from a time when, at eight years old, I was standing at a bus stop beside my now departed paternal grandmother (Granny Murray), who had chronic pain almost all of her life from being hit by a lorry as a young girl. As she exclaimed about her back hurting while waiting for the bus – there was no bench at our bus stop – I felt my own back ache too. I thought this was normal. At thirteen, I had debilitating growing pains in both my arms and legs, which I was assured were to be expected as I grew up. My voice had just dropped – soprano to a tenor no less – and I was growing, so I still thought it was normal. I was kept awake with pain for hours some nights, adopting bizarre contortions – hugging my knees in a tight foetal position helped, and I sprained my left ankle more times than anyone I knew. Still I thought this was normal. I'd always been able to pop my left thumb out of joint as a party trick, and at sixteen I gained the ability to do it with the other thumb too. I could dislocate my left collarbone with a shrug, and my shoulders sounded like marbles in a velvet bag. Yet again, I thought this was normal, even reading online that this was to be expected as people got older. Confusingly, at the same time I could cycle up the local mountain every few days and come home with burning legs and fiery lungs from the intense exercise, which was intensely enjoyable until the next day when, as predictably as clockwork, a tide of unnatural exhaustion would wash over me. In an episode immortalised in enthusiastic retelling by my beloved mother, I decided to 'start running', and after some thought about where to go, I jogged down my street and around the neighbourhood. Ten minutes in I was finished, exhausted, breathless and in terrible pain, and that was the first and last time I voluntarily breached nerdy powerwalking pace without a bicycle. Just a year before I had finished a respectable sixth out of twelve runners in an eight-hundred metre race at school during physical education, so my deterioration was steep. Surely, I still thought, it was normal.

As it turned out, it was not normal, and this became painfully clear when I was in my early twenties and my musculoskeletal system started an open revolt. I was here, queer and with joint pain that was moderate to severe. Exercise was punished with crushing fatigue, the kind that when you're lying flat, you're desperate to be more flat somehow, so exhausted you're unable to sleep. Since then, I've learned I have a heritable connective tissue disease, meaning the bits that hold me together don't work very well – I'm too bendy, and my bones aren't held in place. In one word, disability.

Being in pain all the time sucks, a lot, but the social pain brought upon chronically ill people can suck just as much. Young people with mobility aids are often looked upon with suspicion, breaking the social expectation that disability is associated with old age, and as I started to use a cane, then a more useful crutch when walking, I noticed a change in tone. Decades of British and Irish tabloid sensationalism about benefits cheats and disability spongers have distilled themselves into the momentary gaze of passers-by noticing you in the priority seat at the airport or analysing your gait as you trundle back to the car with groceries. Their eyes dart elsewhere when they're spotted, but the realisation that you're under social surveillance is unsettling when it's novel. Disabled people do often get the special treatment, but this exceptional access is usually provided by the lowest bidder, and often at the maximum inconvenience to the user. Try flying with a wheelchair sometime – you'll get some stories out of it if nothing else.

Being in your mid-twenties and knowing you're most likely going to get more exhausted and sorer as you get older is a grim realisation. As I write this book, I'm trying very hard to get out of a long, deep fatigue flare with no obvious cause, and I'm writing for an hour at a time at most, because those are the limits I must set if I don't want the next few days to be even harder. It's tough, but it's made me a lot more selective about what I do, because wasting energy feels much worse when you're on limited reserves.

Even when I'm 'well', I often have to miss things that are important and meaningful for my work, or that would open doors or improve my life. That being said, being forced to pace myself and take things gently sometimes has helped greatly with carving out a fulfilling life outside of work. With a big workload of human rights activities, many of my friends and I often struggle to avoid overworking and burnout, so having a hard limit can be beneficial. However, disabled and chronically ill activists and workers are often left out of larger human rights discussions, especially at national and international level, because the work is simply inaccessible to us. Disability rights are still routinely simplified to healthcare needs and budget allocations, or a yearly week of seminars and institutional tweets. As a result, disability rights activists often have to carve their own paths both in their personal and professional lives, and it has been working alongside these activists that has taught me more about human rights, and the love and solidarity behind this work more than anything else.

Bee brain

In 2007, when I was fourteen years old, I would regularly go for short walks on winter evenings to clear my head. After school, my brain was always fried, zooted, off on leave, and sometimes going for a walk helped. Not enough to get homework done in time, or to focus on things enough to revise, but a little. The strongest memory I have of my adolescence is on one of these walks on a chilly November evening, when I nearly sprained my ankle with a clumsily placed step into the road, and for the next few minutes I could *think*. It felt like my mind was finally seeing with clarity, accurately dialled in after years of autofocus searching fruitlessly on a busted camera. Compared with how foggy my thoughts were before and after, I came home ecstatic. The adrenaline of nearly falling had briefly allowed me to think clearly, to be able to lift the foggy glass I was used to seeing through. Of course, I hadn't the first clue what had happened.

Sitting at a coffee shop in February 2019, a friend – whom I will call Catherine – and I were talking about our lives and our work, catching up after a long time apart. After telling me about her recent graduation from university in the US, she asked me how I was doing. 'Stressed' was my reply. A year earlier, Catherine had had her eyes opened to a new side of her brain by a university pal, leading to a diagnosis of attention deficit hyperactivity disorder (ADHD), a breakthrough which had turned her life upside down. From failing classes and missing crucial deadlines, feeling constantly overwhelmed and rejected, she was now able to succeed at what she wanted to do, at least most of the time. She still had her bad days, and she still had her very bad days, but she had good days among them. She seemed to be distracted as I talked.

Her eyes narrowed as I answered her questions about my stress, and she asked me to look back on the years we had known each other. Puzzled but open to the idea, we examined all the big things I had tried to do over the years and failed at. Failing spectacularly at subtlety, I asked if she was asking if *I* had ADHD too – a clumsy question, all too easy to plausibly deny. Despite her protestations at my accusation, when we got up to pay for our drinks and head home our separate ways, Catherine admitted that yes, she was convinced I *did* have the same type of brain as her.

I was not convinced. I had been mentally ill most of my teenage years and had assumed that the lingering depression and anxiety from those years was what was shaking the bees that lived in my head. I woke up the next day with my laptop screaming its low battery alarm, desperate to recharge. On the screen were a half dozen web browser tabs with ADHD information and resources on them – it was clear I had gone home, started researching, got completely focused on it for hours, and then succumbed to sleep at some point. I was already late for work, but after some very delayed breakfast I got back into it.

Everything started making sense. My disorganised life, the constant stress of everything being late and going wrong, the hypersensitivity to rejection and criticism, a devastatingly bad sense of time, sensory overload, distraction, hyperfocus on what I was interested in, and two dozen other tendencies of mine all fell into context, and I understood for the first time in my life what to do about it. After a month of talking to others online, reading everything I could and documenting my own experiences, I finally phoned my doctor for an appointment.

ADHD services in Northern Ireland for adults are overwhelmed. Services for children are too, but the adult waiting list was several years, according to my GP. I was initially denied a referral to the service – instead being told to just try to focus more and get more sleep. I said I could afford a private referral, and just weeks later I walked out with my diagnosis papers, very high scores in the brain bee assessment and an empty bank account.

Getting started on ADHD medication is an experience I have found a lot of metaphors for, which is very useful when you're writing a book, but the most poignant experience was an hour after my first dose. I remembered that cold November walk a decade before and my eyes welled up with tears. For the second time in my life, I had the same clarity.

Since that day, I've had good days. Good days are when I can sit down for two or three hours and get things done, organise my surroundings or plan for the future. Medication hasn't been a silver bullet – it rarely is – but the time since has felt like an unrecognisably better life. This wouldn't be clear if you stood in my apartment – it's a clean but desperately messy place – or looked at my email inboxes, but it's a night and day comparison.

Why bring this up? Well, disability shapes the lives we live at every level, whether we recognise it or not, and the clarity that getting support for ADHD has realised has been at least as useful as all the formal and on-the-job education I've had in my work. My neurotype being missed during my school years was a double-edged sword without a doubt – being diagnosed earlier might also have negatively affected how I was treated, but the chaos, stress and grief that this omission resulted in will take a long while to work through. Also, writing a book is perhaps the most daunting task I've ever tried to take on – it's a largely indeterminate project with loose deadlines and sparse guidance compared to most other things, and the end goal is a long way away for most of the process. Being limited to good days means it's taken longer to complete, but as I'll elaborate on later, many of the things I've chosen to write about in these pages would likely not have been completed the same way by a nondisabled person.

IMPORTATNT WORK IN PROGRES!

'She's on Twitter. She's tweeting.'

To the disappointment of everyone in my life, I continue to post on the internet, and have in the past year experimented with new creative outlets to stay grounded and flex my brain cells. This book is something I didn't expect to be writing at such a young age, but it condenses the ideas I've carried around in my head for years. My hope is that it manages to disseminate some of those ideas into your head, where they may bother you also, like an earworm.

Although I'm not young enough to be a genuine 'digital native' as the policy people say – Gretchen McCulloch's excellent book *Because Internet* would define me as a 'full internet person' – I've been online from ten years old and have yet to log off.[1] When you live somewhere where the communities for people like you are covert or absent, the internet is an oasis, and it has consistently been my go-to for community and help since childhood.

Back in my last year of primary school, newly installed computers and a new social network for schoolchildren called Gridclub brought me into online communities for the first time. Being able to customise my homepage, even using rudimentary markup language and HTML, was beyond exciting to my eleven-year-old imagination, and after several failed attempts I was up and running with a GeoCities website filled with animated GIFs and scrolling text just like the best web designers. The next few years were marked by online forums for fans of electronics, bicycles, radios and LGBTQ communities, and I joined what are now the modern social platforms relatively early: YouTube in 2006, Facebook in 2007 and Twitter in 2008. Twitter has been where I've lived since, and it's what I credit most for leading me into human rights work and into being a 'full internet person'. My language, demeanour and especially my humour have been destroyed, rebuilt and destroyed again by this online childhood and adolescence, but teenage savvy and early exposure have brought far more good than bad.

Although 'social media activism' is often derided as pointless, fruitless work that would be better directed elsewhere, it's a useful form of activism especially when you want to get your foot through the door of other human rights work. I've used social media and the internet as a springboard for my journey into that work right from the start, and if like me you have no relevant college or university education before getting started, social media and the networking it allows for can be a game-changer. Human rights circles can unfortunately closely resemble other areas of society, meaning that inaccessibility, exclusivity, nepotism and discrimination can affect who gets a chance and who doesn't, and social media can help in small ways to alleviate this. Despite its tendency to enable harassment and abuse towards marginalised activists and creators, social media can be an invaluable tool for building the audience of people exposed to your work and recruiting the help and support you need to make it a reality.

However, there are many organised forces which keep human rights circles confined to certain thoughts and campaigns, and which keep certain people from getting seats at important tables. We'll touch on this later.

Sign of the times

I'm writing this book in the midst of the largest planetary event of my lifetime, and not long after the worst grief I've experienced. The murder of a close friend, to whom this book is dedicated, and the isolation of living alone during a protracted global pandemic that endangers disabled people more than most, have deeply influenced what I will be setting out in these pages, and they have affected how I think and feel. Trauma and grief are experiences we all go through, and the harshness of injustice, loss and despair can drive us to be better people, to be kinder people, but the tolls they take on our minds and bodies can't be ignored or romanticised.

For every single person I've talked to at length since COVID-19 spread worldwide, 2020 and 2021 have been devastating. We've watched an unprecedented social trauma unfold and seen the responses of our governments, acting in service of business interests, cause so much needless suffering and death. In 2020 we saw growing social unrest over systemic racism and police violence, continued acceleration of climate change, upheaval in major national governments and an impending sense of doom for many. The year 2021 was similar, with my own part of the world setting heatwave records, the fall of nation states and the determined rise of the far right in Europe once more. Every year is a good year to wade into the waves of human rights work, but the 2020s might be a particularly good time. Whether you are fighting for your own rights, fighting for the rights of those you love and cherish, or fighting alongside communities in solidarity with them, there are countless ways to get started.

Here I should provide a somewhat ironic disclaimer: I am currently on the first substantial break from my work since I started it years ago. Despite loving my work, it is increasingly stressful and hostile, and for my health I needed some time off, which I've been on for around a year now.

My own slip-n-slide into human rights got started in 2013, when I quit my electronics engineering course shortly after coming out as transgender. It was too much to study and transition at the same time – both were demanding the energy of full-time jobs and my chronic illness was beginning to slowly unwrap itself. Despite the advice of friends and family, quitting proved to ultimately be a sensible decision and set the scene for a change in life. In 2014, a second life change came along, when I adopted my first cat, who would go on to change the lives of many people. Let's talk about him before the dark stuff. He was called Bilbo before I ever met him.

feelign............. silly

at the ,end of an day, im just a bboy

CHAPTER THREE

Bilbo the Cat

I grew up in a dog family – and one that always ended up with dogs of the same breed, the beautiful mix of cocker spaniels and collies – and had few experiences with cats before adulthood. Other than seeing a few aloof neighbourhood cats in their perches, or the feral cats on my family's dairy farm in the Northern Irish countryside, my exposure to feline friends was mostly through the internet. Although I had little exposure to cats, I didn't consciously love or loathe them either; I had no reason to. The extent of my anti-cat bigotry was agreement with the myth that dogs loved their owners more than cats did, probably because their love was often more evident from across the street, if only to an unexperienced eye. My first proper introduction to a cat in its own home that I recall was when I met Marie, the temperamental cat of my late friend Lyra McKee. I had been forewarned by Lyra, her mother and our mutual friends that Marie was a handful and may make her displeasure known with her well-maintained claws. I perched on Lyra's bed beside her, and she was polite and patient, her mottled tortoiseshell fur standing poofed up and her big eyes clearly cautious. Despite her initial coldness, she gradually moved to accepting gentle pets on the head after an hour or so. Knowing her reputation for being firm with boundaries, I was careful, but her propensity to violence didn't bubble to the surface that day. Marie was her own cat, and she set her own rules and expectations for every situation she found herself in, but she was lovely. In fact, this quality of hers made her more lovely. My anti-cat bias showed its first crack.

The internet should be held accountable for myriad horrors, but anti-cat bigotry is unlikely to be one of them. When I met Marie, I was barely a year into adulthood, and I was still very much in the closet. Not being able to talk openly about my identity led me to exploring quietly on a number of LGBTQ forums online, gradually taking in the information I'd need to come out and learning about queer language, culture and community. This was something I had been researching on and off for years, whenever I could get around internet filters at school and by following the less-than-ideal coverage of LGBTQ people in the news during the 2000s. The emergence of Twitter allowed me to follow normal queer people's lives – their interests, opinions and daily experiences shown authentically and with character – and to slowly learn about what their lives looked like in the UK and Ireland. For my sins I joined the site in 2008, and although all of my tweets and replies prior to 2016 are archived in a ZIP archive hazmat suite on my computer, it provided an incredible source of comfort and solace during some of my loneliest years. A lot of the people I found there had cats, and they were very keen on showing those cats to the world. Despite the limitations of Twitter in the earlier days, my timeline was always full of links to image hosting sites showing photos of felines, and slowly the idea in my head that I wasn't a cat person became quieter and quieter. Though I saw many, the story of one friend's dear cat in particular showed how deep and mutual their love for each other was, and how intermingled their daily lives were as they grew closer together. Over months of smiling at playful photos and reading stories about their pets' naughtiness and character, I found a new and unfamiliar fondness growing within me, and my hesitancy was gradually evaporating. Almost completely without my conscious knowledge, I found myself wanting a cat of my own.

Bilbo belonging

It was a few years before I saw Bilbo for the first time, when I joined a housemate and friend who adopted Bilbo's brother Toulouse as a kitten. Toulouse was one of a litter of four, divided evenly between bright ginger and an oaky brown. All four were happily playing when we visited, and their diminutive size made their growing personalities all the more pronounced. They were well taken care of, playful and energetic, keenly exploring their new world. The instant I saw Bilbo with his ginger-nut fur and his bright white shirt and socks, I had to have him, and I brought him home a short time later. Bilbo was the name given by his mother's owners, and I never had the thought to change it – I had heard at some point that it was bad luck to change an animal's name anyway, and I still find it difficult to discard those kinds of superstitions. Bilbo came home into my three-storey house, and we quickly got to know one another. As a first-time cat owner, I had a steep learning curve to understand how to take care of him, and after some mistakes I slowly found a setup that worked for him. Growing up as any cat does, he steadily developed the character and prance he has today, gradually exploring outside, as he became stronger and wiser, allowing him to find his own way in his world.

Bilbo quickly became a focal point of my Twitter account, and his photos were – and still are – the most popular thing I would upload on any given week. Being stuck at home more and more due to illness and having a passable smartphone camera and reliable internet access made updating my followers on his antics an accessible way to be creative, and a collection of fans began to follow along for his antics. In May 2017, I was becoming a little concerned that some of those who followed me for my developing human rights work would be put off by endless cat photos on their timelines, and asked if people would like him to have his own account. Despite this concern turning out to be unfounded – they wanted more Bilbo, not less – the consensus was that his own online home would be best. I signed him up, accidentally setting his birthday to his birth year of 2014, making him three years old according to Twitter and therefore logging on a full decade before he became old enough to use the platform. Although the automatic ban that resulted was a far from stellar start to his new online career, it was resolved before long, and he started his online exploration. Slowly and surely, his following grew, and by January 2018 he had reached a thousand friends. By this time, I had mostly developed his way with words, a mix of clumsy grammar and typing inaccuracies, which are portrayed as the outcome of having to type with large paws on human keyboards, a user interface never designed for boys like him. Although his tweets today are now all captioned with plain English versions, his style guide is deliberate and relatively consistent, using transcription errors (yellign), patterns with commas (,,,,), emotive all-caps to show EXCITEMENT, and a keen kindness towards those who follow him. The balance I aim for is readability combined with a unique voice that's instantly recognisable, and a dependable character that genuinely reflects how he acts in real life – excited, demanding, comfortable and deeply loving. Distinct from previous dialects like LOLcat ('I Can Has Cheezburger?') and other past and contemporary meme formats,[1] Bilbo's language is closer to the style of some Millennial and Generation Z Twitter users in the deliberate but seemingly careless use of mistakes. Coming back to McCulloch's *Because Internet*, it's similar to how many internet users will craft their 'keysmashes' (asdkhasfjgaskdh) to express strong emotions with deliberation, often going back over these apparently random strings to finesse their appearance and character.[2] These keysmashes, like other common informal writing styles seen online, such as tweets in all-lowercase, often take *more* effort than typing 'properly' – for example, when smartphone autocorrect systems try to remedy these fixes every time they're made. Just as these informal writing styles are deliberated by and for a specific group of people, Bilbo's tweets are crafted for those who enjoy this sort of pseudo-careless style.

It takes a lot more effort to tweet like Bilbo on a smartphone than on a desktop keyboard.

Bilbo's style also extends to the photos he sends out into the world, which are chosen to best show his emotions and character, from a side-eye grumble at being denied a second breakfast or wide-eyed joy on seeing me return home from work. A complicated lore has developed around his online persona since his account's creation. The fact that he is *never* wet after being out in the rain or the state of his harmonious (or otherwise) relationships with the inanimate objects in my apartment form a sizeable proportion of the interactions his fans have with him. His followers caught on quickly that he loves the green bathmat and hates the vacuum cleaner – two things many cat owners will find familiar – but also that my favourite chair is really *his* chair and that the cat-sized version of it is really *my* chair. They remember these 'plot points' even when I forget them, and my own personal Twitter account is regularly overwhelmed by Bilbo's defenders when I dare criticise him for anything in particular. I call him dirty; I'm accused of libel. I tell him off for making a mess, I'm reminded of my own fallibility. These are all deeply silly things, but they do bring people joy.

By July 2017, Bilbo had five thousand followers, and he finished off the year with over ten thousand. His online activity is designed to bring joy and calm to people's lives in little ways – a shot of serotonin as they doomscroll their timeline at 4 a.m. His love and kindness brings a little contentment and peace into people's lives, and it appears that the corner of the internet where cats post tweets is a lot more meaningful and healing than it may first appear.

The cat account in question

One of the great joys and perils of the internet is that you can all too easily become the main character, if only for a brief moment. As Bilbo's account grew, his audience expanded exponentially, and he became a more frequent target of all the sort of nonsense that Twitter can generate. Some of this can be frightening – being stalked online is a horrible experience – and some can be deeply, deeply funny.

In January 2019, Hbomberguy – internet moniker of online gamer Harry Brewis – organised a charity fundraising stream in aid of Mermaids, an organisation that supports trans and questioning children, young people and their families in England, Scotland and Wales.[3] Mermaids had seen new funding from the Big Lottery for their support work put at risk by anti-trans campaigners complaining to the funder, organised in part by former comedy writer Graham Linehan. As Harry set out, the stream was initially planned out of spite for Linehan, and as the event got underway it quickly spiralled to a scope beyond what Harry ever predicted, leading to a global audience of hundreds of thousands and a similar six-figure amount raised for Mermaids.[4] Harry had committed to playing the Nintendo 64 game Donkey Kong, achieving a 101 per cent competition score before he ended his fundraising. This is a lofty goal for one sitting, and after the first day he was forced to sleep, during which a 'Skeleton Crew' of other creators, trans activists and public figures took the opportunity to talk about their work and the issues affecting their communities. This continued at pace for the remainder of the fundraising campaign, including when he was awake, and it was at this point that I was invited aboard to speak. As I sat in a group voice call with large internet personalities and public figures, Bilbo jumped on my lap. He smashed his head into my microphone, sat down and began to purr, loudly. His introduction in front of tens of thousands of people brought a welcome levity to the topics I was talking about, and it marked his first big break. I dropped his Twitter details, and his following began to explode. Later in the month, Patrick Harvie MSP (Member of the Scottish Parliament) presented a motion to congratulate Hbomberguy on his success and included two examples of the guests who appeared on his stream.[5] The outcome of the work of an enterprising parliament worker, the examples were US Congresswoman Alexandria Ocasio-Cortez and 'Northern Irish trans icon and campaigner, Bilbo the Cat'. Bilbo's mention in the motion prompted the question, 'Do European data protection regulations apply to animals, and would his consent need to be obtained before he was included?' – a wonderful detail I love remembering. This small nod to the niche internet community of Twitter cats did not go by unnoticed, and is now marked forever in Hansard, the official parliamentary record. This motion delighted Twitter, and the delight was only intensified when an anti-trans organisation in Scotland suggested that Harvie was invoking sectarian tension in Northern Ireland because Bilbo's Twitter profile mentioned him being an 'orange boy'.[6] This is, as you might expect, a reference to the colour of his fur as seen in the visible spectrum and not a designation of his social upbringing in the context of the decades of civil conflict in Northern Ireland. In now long-deleted tweets, this group thoroughly embarrassed themselves to an audience of tens of thousands, insisting that

Bilbo – 'the cat account in question', as the accusations referred to him – was unpicking the fragile peace process in my part of the world. This predictably made Twitter extremely animated for several days, after which Bilbo had found even more friends.

By the time he turned six years old in August 2020, he had amassed over a hundred thousand followers, a core set of whom follow his every adventure. Bilbo had stolen the hearts of tens of thousands of people from hundreds of countries and had been featured in places as diverse as the Scottish Parliament, NPR and the *New York Times*.[7] His friends were writing him letters, sending him presents and painting watercolour portraits, and he was bringing joy to their hearts in return. Known online as @thegoodcatboy, he was unquestioningly living up to his username, but he wasn't the only bboy in the game.

CCATNIP CATNIP CANTNIP

CHAPTER FOUR

Cat Twitter

On the internet, nobody knows you're a dog. Anonymity and flexibility have long been some of the best and worst features of social networks like Twitter, allowing for whistleblowing and protection from persecution in equal measure as facilitating harassment, intimidation and abuse. There is a plethora of accounts for pets and animals on the site, but cats have been part of internet culture for much longer than Twitter has existed. From the early days of ASCII text artwork, on to animated GIFs and image macros like LOLcats, cats and their expressive faces have been a bountiful resource for web surfers for decades now. When I was finding my online footing for the first time at home, 'I Can Has Cheezburger?' and countless similar memetic formats served as vectors for humour on forums everywhere. Their language of getting the order and spelling of words wrong is basic, but when it's done well it can be a durable form of humour. This transferred to Twitter as the site emerged as a major platform, and Bilbo was a long way from the first cat account signed up. Claire Belton and Andrew Duff's Pusheen comic cat came on the scene in May 2010, and Nyan Cat took the world by storm the following year. Today, cats on the internet post daily videos to YouTube, provide an outlet for genuine emotion on several platforms and serve as reaction GIFs both for and against reply guys everywhere.

Cat Twitter is a loose collection of accounts on the platform which present themselves as written by the cats featured. They usually feature one or two animals at most – animal shelter and sanctuary accounts are substantially different in their cause and effect – and they're usually operated by their human owner. Although there are cat accounts in dozens of languages, the most common and most popular ones tweet in English, though often a variably garbled form at best. @PépitoTheCat has been around for the majority of Twitter's existence and has posted regularly with webcam photos of him leaving or returning to his home through his cat flap. His fans appropriately wish him safety on his voyages or warm welcomes home, en masse, every time a tweet is triggered. The connection people have with Pépito is through the real-time nature of his photos – when you can see his head, he's coming home and when you can see his tail, he's on his way out to explore.

Other accounts have followed a cat's life from the moment they're adopted to the moment they pass away, featuring an entire life cycle of love and grief, and introducing some complicated emotions to their followers and some ethical considerations for those running accounts. Much like followers' own pets, or the pets of friends, when a cat you've known online for some time dies, there can be a sharing of that collective grief across all their online friends. This brings us to the first uncomfortable reality of Cat Twitter – the friends and followers they amass, being human, are much more likely to outlive them than the other way around.

Love and loss

Peepee of Peepee's Playhouse (@peepeeplayhouse) was a kind and characterful member of Cat Twitter, with a large following and many caring friends. When he passed away in April 2019 from health complications, many of his hundred thousand followers shared in the grief of his owner, expressing genuine, sincere and significant grief. When Peepee went over the rainbow, a small part of tens of thousands of people's lives did too. His account has stayed online as a memorial to the humour, joy and comfort he brought to so many. He was just a litle creacher.[1]

When I talk about the emotions people have for internet cats, it's not uncommon for people from outside this corner of the internet to respond with ridicule. Without a doubt, following a cat online and sharing in the silly community that surrounds them every few days is a far cry from caring for and growing up with a cat you're responsible for, but the vicarious feelings that their followers experience are genuine and appear to have significant effects on the well-being and lives of many of them. Whether it's introducing them to cats and helping them pluck up the courage to adopt one themselves or simply giving them funny faces to look at when they're having a sleepless night, these seemingly juvenile Twitter accounts do affect people for the better.

As part of a YouTube project I published in 2019, titled 'Cat Twitter', I put together a survey of the proprietors of cat accounts and of the followers they had. Over thirty account owners provided answers to me, and 450 cat account fans gave their input also.[2] The data I gathered through this were an approximate representation of the followers who interact most with some of the more common cat accounts, from across many countries, age groups, genders and cat owner experiences.

The stories I heard from account owners featured mostly marginalised people finding safe outlets online through the pets they loved dearly, and the stories from followers expressed everything from simply wanting cute cats on their timelines to following as an escape from an increasingly stressful, hostile and unwelcoming world. Individuals with depression, suicidal thoughts and other mental health problems had dedicated Twitter accounts just for calming down with the communities of cats they collected on their timelines, and others still used the accounts to deal with loneliness or the recent loss of their own pets. From the tens of thousands of words of responses I've read, from hundreds of people, Cat Twitter is clearly an important source of relief, respite and repose in a world they feel unwelcome in. A surprising number of younger fans suggested following cats on Twitter helped them get some time away from issues overwhelmingly affecting people their age like future income security or climate catastrophe. One individual said they found internet cats when they got online for the first time after a devastating hurricane. I'm not even close to being qualified to assess these responses for their deeper meaning, but

I'm inclined to believe what people contributed of their own free will.

These emotions are regularly reflected in the private messages cat accounts receive, from thanking the cat for getting them through a difficult week to expressing their grief at the loss of their own.

Looking at the raw numbers, six in ten respondents said that Cat Twitter helped their well-being a lot, with just under an additional four in ten saying it helped a little. A handful said they weren't affected, and two said it hurt them a little, though it's unclear why. Of course, Cat Twitter is likely to replicate the problems of Twitter and internet communication generally, and the responses I received demonstrated that clearly.

Cat counselling

If my mental health had a credit score, I'd doubt it would get a mortgage. Bilbo has become one of the best things for my well-being from day to day, because caring for, loving and being loved by a cat can be outstandingly rewarding and healing. I talk to Bilbo every day, and he knows when I need company and sits on me for hours. He's a very effective nurse.

No one has quite figured out how to let a cat tweet what it wants to say, so for now, a human is involved at some point. Although people often do experience significant emotions from getting to know a cat online, the way they interact with them will usually go via that person. This means that some cat account owners receive a lot of messages detailing grief, trauma, mental health problems and other subjects that they may not be expecting or equipped to process.

In my survey, a great majority of account owners said their Twitter presence helped them a lot, and none said it hurt them. When asked to detail why they tweeted as their cat, their reasons chimed with my own for Bilbo's account – they loved their cats an inordinate amount and wanted to share them with the world, and they enjoyed the interactions they had with other cats on the platform and with their larger following. For many, myself included, the hobby allows for a daily escape from highly stressful work, and for others from tense situations at home. Others found running their cat's account helped them process difficult things going on in their life, relieve loneliness and restore their faith in humanity due to the sheer positivity and happiness communicated from their cat's followers.

When you're struggling with something in life, it helps to have an outlet for that, to be able to talk to someone about your problems, or to have a friendly face to turn to when things get bad. I have a PO box where people can send me physical mail, and in the two years I've operated it, I've received hundreds of letters, cards and packages addressed to my cat. Some of them have been simple cards saying hello, and some of them have been multiple-page handwritten letters, spilling the heart of the writer out and asking the cat for comfort. Despite being sent to a human being's PO box, they were addressed to the cat, written for the cat and worded as if whispered to that cat lying on their chest while they cried at night. I've been astounded by the beauty and emotion that goes into a lot of the letters I receive, and they've been an important thing to consider when presenting Bilbo online. Many other cat account operators said how the messages that they get are the most intense part of the process, both positively and negatively. Some said that they are inundated with pictures of other people's cats, celebratory news and messages of love, and others said they receive messages of grief about the loss of their own cat, about homesickness, and indeed about how their cat account has helped people deal with mourning, abuse and suffering. Again, the theme of using Cat Twitter accounts as a vector for emotional outpouring was common, and the messages sent demonstrated a profound meaningfulness behind their interactions.

Although it's now something I look back on as quite funny, the response of anti-trans activists to Bilbo being recognised in the Scottish Parliament led to an individual attempting – and thankfully failing – to find personal and sensitive information about me online. I was alerted by Twitter, my personal website and other platforms that someone was attempting to brute-force their way into my accounts, and although I had prepared for that eventuality, this was an unwelcome stress for several days. Although doxing (the finding and releasing of private personal information, usually online) is uncommon on Cat Twitter, there is a rational fear of it among many account operators, who were shown in my research to be disproportionally from minority communities and at higher risk than most of being doxed.

tthe early boy....... gets the milk

There is no ethical tweeting

When does posting about your cat on Twitter become unethical? Is there a point where showing your much-loved pet to the world becomes exploitative or harmful to it, or to those who follow along from their own accounts? In my research, a small number of Cat Twitter fans said they did worry about the well-being of some cats, but that they trusted that the vast majority were well taken care of and free of exploitation for the camera. Others worried that the growth of accounts would lead to an increase in owners bothering their cats more to participate. In the main, Cat Twitter account operators are run by people who adore their cats and who take care of them well, and their followers are cat lovers in turn. Cat well-being, therefore, should be pretty high up the community's priority list, and this comes through in some of the messages both Bilbo and others receive.

There will always be a spectrum of what people think acceptable for interacting with cats, and a similar, if not even wider, spectrum of what the cats themselves find acceptable. My own boy Bilbo is cuddly and affectionate, and he loves playtime and rough pets on the kitchen floor. Others will give you free arm surgery for petting them the wrong way or in the wrong place. Part of the joy and communication that comes with owning and raising cats is the mutual language that develops between the cat and their human, the boundaries they negotiate and the behaviour that signals what everyone wants. If I pat my lap twice, Bilbo will jump up if he wants, knowing he's welcome to at the time. If Bilbo rolls onto his back and tucks his paws up into his chest, it means I am allowed two, maybe three belly rubs, and he'll pretend to swat me away if he wants to stop. This nuanced communication doesn't come across well on such a short-form platform as Twitter, which can lead to misunderstandings and stress. When Bilbo was ill in 2020, he received hundreds of concerned messages from his fans wishing him well, and several alleging that I had mistreated him, which were upsetting to read through. Over the course of our years together, I've learned that Bilbo likes both his cuddles and his own space, much like myself, so we coexist harmoniously, as happy to be at opposite ends of the room as intertwined in a snuggle. The rules I've established are that Bilbo is only ever on camera if he wants to be, and he goes where he likes, so if I'm streaming on Twitch and he's on camera but wants to explore outside, he gets to go out unless there's a very good health or safety reason why he shouldn't. Cats are extremely good at teaching boundaries and consent, and it takes both time and context to explain this to communities of followers online. Ultimately, this is an exercise of trust between us and our cats, and us and our Twitter followers – and all of this is before we even discuss what relationships can develop between these different groups.

A parasocial relationship is where one party is deeply invested in and knowledgeable about the other party, or believes themselves to be, while the other party only knows of them in passing or not at all.[3] These relationships have existed in various forms for centuries but came to prominence through mass media exposure and celebrity in the twentieth century. Superfans of famous musicians, followers of the royal family who wait outside hospitals to see the royal baby, and fans who engage with every

YouTube video by a large creator can be described as experiencing this sort of relationship. These imbalances in knowledge and power aren't inherently damaging – it's natural for a popular Twitch streamer to not know all their fans and for many of their followers to be big fans of their work – but as follower counts grow, it is more likely for harmful dynamics to emerge.

When you have tens or hundreds of thousands of followers somewhere on the internet, the vast majority will go by without interacting with your content unless your tweet's a real banger. It's normal for a small minority to interact with a lot more of your work, and it's this that I enjoy most about Cat Twitter. This group of people are overwhelmingly kind and positive and want the best for the cat and their owner, and they demonstrate that clearly in how they interact with people online. As other cat account owners communicated through responses to my survey and in my own experience, there can be a small number of people who charge through established boundaries, have unreasonable demands and demonstrate a complete disdain for the feelings and safety of those they're talking to. Experiences others detailed included insisting on home addresses, stalking and sexual harassment, all of which I've also experienced. This dampens a lot of the joy of the hobby and can make account owners increasingly wary of interacting with fans and followers. Since Bilbo passed ten thousand followers, I have tightened my online security, been more guarded about revealing my home address and introduced screening for letters received at my PO box. One regrettable outcome of online parasocial relationships like these is the interpretation by this minority of interaction and short messages from you as personal closeness or suggestiveness, when in reality you're just answering a question about how long you've owned your pet. It's all very stressful.

However, these experiences can teach account owners and others working in the public eye valuable lessons about security, safety and personal boundaries, and they are lessons best learned early on. My advice to anyone who has, or hopes to have, a significant following online is to assume someone will try to barge their way into every account you own, and that if you can reset your passwords with your email address, make well sure that email account has the best security settings you can tolerate. Two-factor authentication is easier than ever, and it should be your standard, starting today. The peace of mind that this brings can help a lot to make Cat Twitter – which should ideally be a happy and carefree place – feel a lot like it hopes to be.

Coming and going

I'm not sure how long Cat Twitter will be around. I'm not sure how long Twitter will be around, really. Bilbo won't be online for ever, and neither will I, or you. Right now, he enjoys a vibrant community of fans who enthusiastically talk with him regularly, and of whom a minority are funnelled towards the rest of what I do: human rights work. Although Twitter has been fertile ground for important social movements, minority community formation, art and speech, it's also been victim to exploitation by misinformation, propaganda and societal harm. At the same time as countless friendships have been formed, helping hands offered and education provided on the platform, far-right hate groups have flourished, vaccine disinformation has exploded and minority groups have been driven apart. The platform's crackdown on misinformation and the far right – with varying degrees of success – is promising, but far from ensures it as a place of value for cat fans and human rights workers alike.

For all its flaws, Twitter (and Cat Twitter specifically) has been a wonderfully positive influence on my human rights work, and my ability to reach bigger audiences with whom to share it. As interest in human rights issues grows among younger and more internet-savvy generations, I have great hope that the work human rights defenders do has a bright future.

tthere is a stranger . in my house

CHAPTER FIVE

Human Rights?

I want to ask a few questions of you before we get started on the meat of this chapter. What, to you, is a meaningful change in your life and the world? It could be something for you personally, like getting your car's tyres replaced before the slippery winter roads appear, or something for you and yours, like checking your grandmother's car to make sure it's roadworthy for the winter. It could be something for your society, like lobbying your local government to grit the roads, or for national regulators to prevent imports of substandard tyres. You could look wider, to the landmass you're on, the continent you're a part of, or the planet you inhabit.

What do you feel in your heart about the world today? If you're reading this shortly after publication, then perhaps you are feeling excitement at the end of the COVID-19 pandemic? Anxiety about political violence, global instability, about poverty, climate change? Hope for the world you've just imagined? How long have you felt these feelings, and why did they come about?

Has anything happened in the recent past that's changed your thoughts on the world? Maybe the Black Lives Matter movement in the US, or the Russian invasion and war in Ukraine? Is there a housing crisis where you live, or have you experienced heatwaves or flooding like you've never seen before? What are you worried about, and what do you want to change?

What does a better world look like to you? Thinking outside the box of political feasibility and financial cost for a moment, imagine a society – locally, nationally, globally – that you'd be truly happy to be a part of. Are people fulfilled in their lives? Do they have to pay for their healthcare, for their home? Do they have to get a visa to visit a dying family member in another country? Do countries even exist anymore? Do global superpowers still toy with the balance of world peace and conflict? Is there a stock market? How many hours do people work a day? How much are they paid, or do they have to do paid work at all? How's the climate looking, do people still drive cars and eat meat? If you have or want children, are you excited for their future?

Who made your dream world the way it is? Did you singlehandedly change the law, or maybe dictatorship fell to social uprisings around the world? Was it people fighting for their own rights who changed the world for the better, or those speaking for others who had been ignored? Those with money and power, or those without?

What do human rights abuses even mean in your dream world? They may not even be concerns in this utopia, eradicated like smallpox. If they are still pressing issues, they may be understood in a completely new way, with our tendency to compartmentalise and silo human rights issues apart from each other seen as infantile and primitive.

Does this world feel a long way away?

I find myself thinking about these sorts of things occasionally, perhaps to motivate myself, perhaps to escape reality for a moment. I imagine you do a version of this from time to time yourself, perhaps hoping for better housing or escaping from the latest reports from the International Panel on Climate Change. When I think about human rights and activism, I find it useful to imagine like this to reset the limits in my own head about what things are possible. If you have been involved in many forms of activism recently, you may have experienced burnout, hopelessness, despair. For many activists in the present moment, especially those working in areas of active conflict and countries descending into authoritarianism, standing still would feel like progress. Treading water is still better than drowning. I've felt similar – the demonisation of discussions on human rights in the UK has accelerated in recent years,[1] and in particular, I've found my own focus of trans activism constantly in a hostile spotlight – but I also find thinking bigger like this can be a brief salve from the endless drudgery of what we currently find ourselves fighting against.

Incrementalism can feel comforting. The prospect of making small but tangible gains towards a better future is attractive, and it has seen success as a method in many examples in recent world history, especially in the area of thematic human rights like disability, sexual orientation and gender. It can also be limiting though, because when incremental progress is seen as the only possibility, that your country or region can only achieve what 'better' parts of the world are doing and not more, it can relegate the ultimate goal to naïve utopianism.

Utopianism can feel comforting too. Dreaming big and making daring moves to achieve those objectives feels noble, worthwhile and righteous. It can work to various degrees – decolonisation efforts across African nations in the twentieth century are examples of this – but it is also likely to be frustrated by the societal forces that human rights defenders currently contend with. The balance of power in the world tends to prefer incrementalism, conservativeness and patience, and many utopian dreams for a better world have fallen victim to these constraints. For instance, left-wing governments in Latin America have been regularly overthrown since the 1960s by US-backed military and authoritarian regimes using torture and violence to protect business interests and prevent the spread of democracy, socialism and human rights.[2]

Dreaming big is human – there's a reason we do so much of it as children and teenagers – but without preparation and strategy, both the efforts and the successes will be vulnerable, weak. It requires many people taking many paths and, using their combined strength and skills, working to make their goals a reality – in a word, solidarity.

I still think about utopias, both because they're comforting and because I think it's fundamentally human to want to live in peace. This approach is easy to write off as overly emotional, childish or lacking nuance, which on its own it may be. After all, the world we inhabit is indescribably complex, made only more so by centuries of colonisation, conflict and the mess left behind afterwards. I believe most people want to live happy and peaceful lives, and I consider efforts to make other people's lives happier and more peaceful tomorrow inseparable from human rights.

There's no one way to get started in human rights work; there's not even a good definition of what 'human rights work' actually encompasses. In my opinion, there's similar merit in making sure your friend has a roof over their head tonight as there is in speaking at the Human Rights Council at the UN. One's playing the short game and the other the long one, and they both have their place. Although I won't be providing an A-to-Z manual on human rights work – I'm not capable of doing so and I doubt many are – I do hope to distil some ideas about how you might make the world a little better for you and yours, and indeed for theirs and ours.

If you're not new to this sort of thing, thanks for what you do. It's only due to the work of other human rights defenders that I've been able to get involved, and I owe you a debt of gratitude.

Getting new tyres as the snow rolls in might keep you out of a deadly car crash, which is a good thing for you, your loved ones and society at large. Insulating your house lowers your carbon footprint over time and helps the global effort in a small way. However, I would advise being wary of overreliance and naïve faith in personal efforts in changing society and the world. The ideology of individualism grown from the twentieth-century myths of the American Dream has been adopted and weaponised to limit what is and isn't seen as feasible, where responsibility lies for the world's problems, and what can and ought to be done to solve them. Just as Reaganomics in the US and Thatcherite politics in the UK dissolved expectations that the state provide for its people while simultaneously privatising profits, many human and civil rights issues have had the burden of their solution left to individuals, regardless of how devastating their effects are to societies at large.[3] Petrochemical companies lobby for recycling schemes and renewable heating schemes to protect their image and deflect attention from their own impacts on the environment while reaping record profits, despite being among the first to forecast global climate change in the 1960s and 70s.[4] Financial collapse caused by multinational banks means millions have to suffer austerity in public spending and a social expectation to start tugging on your bootstraps, while those same banks see bailouts and immunity.

Upon my first undertakings in human rights work, I quickly learned how human rights – the way we talk about them, what we consider rights and privileges, and who we see as deserving and undeserving – are a product of, and inseparable from, the social hierarchies established around the world over the past several hundred years. This isn't exactly a difficult perspective to establish, but it's one often excluded when talking about the specific problems of the world we find ourselves in today. During the 2020 lockdown – well, the first one – I started cycling every day, for an hour a day. The order came in late March from each of the devolved governments across the UK that we were only allowed out for essential shopping, work and exercise, with an hour being the upper limit of what was considered a reasonable bicycle ride. Picking up on my long-abandoned Audible account, I began using this hour to get round to books that I'd been trying to read for years. I've always struggled with this, my attention span and fatigue playing havoc with any real prospect of committing to a long read, but the stimulation of a bicycle ride and an audiobook mixing softly with the background noise of traffic led to the most reading yet in my adult life. I began with the works of David Graeber, an anarchist anthropologist who sadly passed away in 2020, and went on to the works of Naomi Klein. Klein's writing on climate change and activism were enthralling, but the work of hers which left the most indelible mark on me was *The Shock Doctrine*. In it, she explores how countries around the world have been raided and pillaged under the guise of free market capitalism and how torture and abuse shaped endless wars in the Middle East and Latin America, among much more.[5] *The Shock Doctrine* is stomach-churning, and it's a rough read at times, but it is an excellent antidote to the poison many of us in human rights work are fed that our issues are separate and unconnected, to be addressed in silos without looking back to learn from history or from lessons taught elsewhere. Our contemporary issues – war, climate change, the rights of thematic groups like women, LGBTQ people, disabled people – are discussed in media and public discussion as discrete, independent fights, or if they do interact, as at odds with each other. Looking back over just the past few decades proves otherwise, and learning about the successes of the past – against seemingly insurmountable challenges like the US-backed dictatorships in Latin America – is a deeply valuable tool for figuring how your human rights work fits into the bigger picture of tomorrow's history.

Becoming jaded with the world isn't the answer, but a cautious and critical approach to why society works the way it does is crucial. Warrantless faith in law and order, societal norms or human rights work as a way to change things can lead you down dangerous paths, as success evades your reach and workloads pile on. Despondence and burnout are likely. I've been severely burned out multiple times, and it's much easier to enter this mental quicksand than it is to recover from it. A critical approach to the work you do and want to do, and about how useful the 'official channels' for change really are, is a tool best to be equipped with early.

I've come across a useful metric for identifying this in budding new activists, and it's entirely relatable, but unfortunately close to home, for many of us who have mental health problems. If, during the past few years, you have felt patronised and infantilised by governments and leaders telling you to protect your mental health while they defund health services, you have a good seed crystal to develop this critical thinking from.

The way things are

While we're at it, human rights defender is very silly language altogether to my ears. I've been calling myself that for years because it's the term used in international law, but it still doesn't feel quite right. So, to be clear, when I say human rights defenders, take this to mean activists, advocates, campaigners, artists, community builders, protesters, carers and medics, professionals, academics, anyone who devotes part of their life to making the world better for people by changing society.

Human rights work can be done by individuals, but it's usually more successful when done as part of a movement, campaign or organisation which brings activists and their supporters together in a way which allows them to organise, share work and mutually support each other. Whether you're entering a movement, either budding or established, or you're trying to start one, what you can, can't, should and shouldn't do will depend heavily on the context you find yourself in, but there are some basic concepts which will help you navigate this new environment.

First of all it's important to remember that the organisations that protect and progress human rights – and the ideas that they incubate and develop – haven't escaped the relentless push for privatisation and individualism that has transformed almost every major market and economy in the world. Civil society organisations – a term meaning non-governmental organisations who work on human rights issues – are often driven by funding applications, corporatised management and public relations policies which significantly tame the work they're able or willing to do. Many a radical (or at least progressive) campaigning organisation has slowly had its political messages and big visions picked apart by business practices and funding requirements, and its methods tamed to fit. The professionalisation of human rights organisations has brought many benefits – stable(-ish) incomes for (some) activists, access to decision makers and those in the corridors of power – but has also fenced off the world their founders fought for.[6] Demands for radical social changes by numerous queer people's organisations – abolition of rent, prisons and police; free healthcare; public housing for all – move to tamer campaigns like specific healthcare services for queer people; protection from discrimination; and protection in employment. Campaigns for marriage equality are perhaps the most well-known example of this, where in Ireland a national referendum was fought between openly anti-LGBTQ groups and 'moderate' LGBTQ groups and coalitions who took a fairly conservative approach, keeping their messaging as palatable and uncontroversial as possible to ensure they got the referendum passed in their favour. Some LGBTQ people are seen by the public as more acceptable than others – something that trans people are negatively affected by in particular – and campaign groups have tended to avoid those less-accepted groups in their messaging. Depending on your politics, you might see this as anything from a pragmatic and sensible approach in a high-stakes, high-visibility environment to an unforgiveable abandonment of those seen as Too Queer for Ireland's middle class.

To be clear, this isn't a rejection of the work done and being done to secure health services for LGBTQ people, for protections in employment or for legal recognition – these are all things which have meaningful and often substantial benefits to many in our communities. However, being *limited* to these sorts of activities can be an impediment to long-term progress, especially when organisations act (or try to be seen to act) outside of wider political discussions, ideology and campaigns. If human beings have a right to safe housing, and if LGBTQ people are disproportionately likely to face housing insecurity or be homeless, it is fundamentally limiting for 'public housing for all' to be off the table as a position to hold.

Part of this tendency to rein in the broad scope of activist aims and objectives comes from, ironically, the formalised aims and objectives which develop during the professionalisation these organisations go through as they search for sustainability and safety. Strategic planning sets out the goals of an organisation so it can organise towards their realisation, but the accompanying recommended institution of political neutrality and pragmatic selective silence for the comfort of funders and political leaders can hamper their ability to bring about these more fundamental changes to society. This is worsened still when funding is provided by the state or the sectors you seek to change, where criticism is seen as political, as ungrateful, as biting the hand that feeds you.

The rise of today's human rights organisations across much of the world was contemporaneous with the rise of state regulation on companies and charities, especially regarding fundraising and employment law. This regulation has again provided benefits to society – the potential eradication of scam charities and corruption, and protection for the labour rights of activists and other employees within these groups. However, charity law in many countries restricts the rights of charities to campaign on certain issues, sometimes prohibiting any activity seen as political or partisan.[7] Is healthcare for a minority group seen as political? To many, yes, but it's deemed acceptable in the context of an advocacy organisation for that group. It's often when charities and non-profits advocate for broader and more fundamental political and social change that regulators start taking notes.

This leaves human rights organisations stuck between a rock and a hard place then – the choice between making sure activists have a roof over their head or allowing them to campaign on the issues most important to their communities is not an easy one to make. These are conflicts I'm very familiar with myself, and not ones I will pretend only happen to other people. Although it is profoundly uncomfortable, I often find myself falling closer than I would like towards comfortable but unfulfilling work than to meaningful but financially unstable work. For many, the conflicting responsibilities to both employees and social progress can be balanced, but not held harmoniously beside each other. This is a result of the context in which we must work, not in the work or people themselves, and I see it as something that must change if human rights are to be meaningfully respected for everyone. Unfortunately, history shows that in most places, but especially regions with unstable politics or a history of conflict, like where I live in Northern Ireland, the adoption of incrementalism in exchange for making rent each month can be hard to avoid for long.

That's a bummer, right? It can seem so, but none of this stops you, me or anyone else from making meaningful differences to the world we inhabit. For many activists, these restrictive practices we must adopt or work within form part of what we want to see change, so that communities can more effectively and safely organise for their own needs. Of course, depending on the work you want to do, you'll benefit or be held back to different degrees by society and its restrictions. Activists fighting for their own rights are often those least listened to, as many campaigns in disability and LGBTQ rights have shown.

Different areas of human rights activism come with histories of different length, intensity and relevance. I'm predominantly a trans rights activist, and although trans rights activists are far from a new thing, trans rights activism as a body of knowledge, achievement and legacy is relatively new; it is less developed than, for example, disability rights activism in many countries. Although this can make progress seem less accessible and more complicated, it can be helpful to have a limited precedent to follow, because you sometimes get to write the handbook. When I started activism work for trans young people in Northern Ireland, there was extremely limited local knowledge in the area, so adopting the good parts of practice from elsewhere, while abandoning the bad parts, was a lot more feasible than joining an established, stable organisation. The balance I've had to strike most often in my work is that between fulfilling and meaningful work and financial stability in life. This is... risky, and the balance needed shifts constantly as we age and grow. However, the absence or scarcity of human rights activism in your area on a given topic is not all bad – it brings opportunities – but it might also be a case of picking your poison.

yuor dinner is not safe form me

Where this all came from

The concept that human beings have certain rights that must be respected has existed since time immemorial. Punishments for murder, sexual crime and theft could be gruesome and vindictive, but they were based in the concept that life, bodily autonomy, and property (at least for those deemed worthy) were deserving of a level of protection by society at large. After all, protecting your social group from death, injury or loss is a self-preservation strategy, one which developed alongside human evolution, and the consequences for those who transgressed these expectations were understood to protect the social group as a whole. Religious and spiritual arguments for the protection of life and property developed in tandem across many world faiths and spiritual frameworks, and the idea of life and other rights protected by divinity became enshrined in both religious and secular law. In what is now the UK, formal rights were extended to the landed gentry and nobility long before the population as a whole, as seen in Magna Carta. Feudalism waned, enclosure stole public common land from the people, and the philosophy of individualism and personal liberty expanded understanding of what the concept of rights encompassed. Rights were, however, not afforded to all, as European colonialism went on to brutally demonstrate. The concept of citizenship emerged as a way to define those with rights, entitlements and responsibilities under the law, but this was restricted to those deemed suitable or deserving by states and rulers. In the past few hundred years, the development of institutions like the Parliament of England into pseudo-democratic mechanisms, and the emergence of democratic governments elsewhere, have further fleshed out the scope of what human rights protect and who is entitled to them. Societies can have very strange ideas of what is and isn't a democratic right – the UK is seen by many as an outstanding example of a democratic society, but we have an unelected upper House of Lords, a monarchy entitled to veto legislation, and an almost complete lack of democracy in the workplaces which form huge parts of our lives.

On the timescale of human civilisation, it is a very recent idea that everyone has unalienable human rights protected by law by the country of which they are a citizen. Although the ideal is preached by many global powers who purport to practise it, this remains a utopian idea not yet fully brought to reality by any government anywhere. There is no country on earth where human rights are experienced by all to their fullest.

Human rights apply to human beings. This, however, comes with a catastrophic vulnerability. If a state or society sees a person or their community as not fully human or as not human at all, they can be abused, tortured and subjected to unfathomable atrocities to protect those who *are* seen as human. The twentieth-century crimes against humanity that constituted the Holocaust were the result of years of campaigns to dehumanise specific social classes and communities. Wholesale destruction of human life – particularly of Jewish, Romani, disabled and LGBTQ people's lives among others – was argued by the Nazi government as necessary to protect society as a whole. The rise of eugenics in the US and the institutional forced sterilisation, segregation, detention and abuse of disabled people, Native Americans and

Black people were similarly argued as necessary for the protection of society. They took much longer to dismantle than to establish and served as the framework for immeasurable suffering during the decades that followed, much of which is within living memory. Of course, the legacy of both of these examples has influenced the world we live in today and will likely continue to do so for generations to come.

This second example is important because the US, while establishing human rights mechanisms around the world, was forcibly sterilising and institutionalising people based on disability, race and ethnicity, and behaviour. When the Universal Declaration of Human Rights was published in 1948, disabled people, for example, were seen as not fully deserving of human rights in many jurisdictions, and to this day numerous states argue that some disabled people ought not to be entitled to make their own decisions or live their lives as they wish. Although human rights law and the mechanisms that use it are important, the question of *who* receives these human rights must be indelible in the heads of human rights defenders. These are some of the most well-known campaigns of dehumanisation in human history but the possibility of them happening again remains a reality, and there are countless other examples of genocide and state oppression from almost every corner of the world in just the past few decades. Although the scenarios you encounter in your life are likely to be less profound than these, it is still important to be conscious of when dehumanisation happens in subtle ways. The worst excesses of human cruelty throughout history have usually grown from popular indifference to rhetoric which, when unchecked, balloons from almost invisible to all-encompassing within mere years. 'Never Again' becoming reality requires continued vigilance, especially at home.

Human rights law

A major keystone for the formal protection of our rights as human beings throughout the world is through international human rights law. The right to life, to speak your mind, to have an identity that's true to yourself, are protected, along with countless others, by a plethora of human rights laws, developed through the twentieth century into a large and complicated nest of rights. All of us have human rights, and in theory they can only be limited where there is good cause, like limiting the freedom of business owners in order to protect their workers or limiting the rights of parents in order to protect their children.

Some of this framework is provided via the United Nations, whereas the various regions of the world have adopted regional mechanisms, like the European Convention on Human Rights (ECHR). Human rights law is then implemented in some form by the countries around the world who ratify it into their own law. It is promoted, progressed and enforced in different ways from state to state, and international bodies have varying levels of authority to monitor and report on compliance.

Human rights can be absolute, where they can never be violated, or qualified, where they can be in defined circumstances. It may surprise some readers to learn that the three absolute rights within the ECHR – the right to freedom from torture, the right to freedom from slavery and the right to no punishment without law – do not include the right to life, which allows for limited use of deadly force. All other rights in the Convention are qualified, meaning they must be balanced alongside the rights of others. A timely example is Article 5 of the ECHR on the right to liberty and security, which has provisions to allow detention to prevent the spread of infectious diseases.

When a government ratifies an international human rights treaty, they are obligated to implement it in different ways depending on the rights in question. For civil rights – the right to vote, the right to assemble and the right to be protected from discrimination, among other things – states are obligated to immediately make changes to law, regulation and policy to ensure they are respected, protected and fulfilled.[8] For economic, social and cultural rights – the right to raise a family, the right to education, the right to an adequate standard of living and the right to social security, among other things – states are obligated to *progressively* enact measures to ensure they are respected, protected and fulfilled, in consideration of the maximum resources available to the state over time. This means that if a country ratifies a treaty, some of its protections will apply at once whereas others may take time.

International human rights law is the broadest tool, in theory protecting every person in the countries which ratify it, but it's also the slowest to be realised, and the slowest to adapt to new developments and changing societies. What takes days for local groups to achieve may take decades for the mechanisms of the United Nations.

Human rights law is just one tool of many at our disposal when advocating for people's rights; it's not perfect and suffers from major flaws. These mechanisms are often based on the assumptions and norms of the Global North, making it prone to resistance elsewhere, seen as an underhand form of neo-colonialism. Treaties are also products of their time, and older law can reflect badly on the era in which it was written. For example, Article 5 of the ECHR also provides for the detention of 'persons of unsound mind', an outdated and offensive term for people with mental health problems and other disabled people. The law moves too slowly for many, and the work that activists do with international law is more likely to have meaningful benefits for people next decade than next week. After all, direct action to block bailiffs is much more likely to keep a roof over a family's head tonight than appealing to the European Court of Human Rights, not least because that option only becomes available after the exhaustion of domestic legal challenges through local and national courts. Although I find international human rights law extremely useful in my work and I appreciate the progress it has enabled towards a society where human rights are fulfilled, it cannot work on its own, both by its design and in the context within which it operates.

This is good for people trying to get involved in human rights work. It's daunting to read about international law for the first time, and for years I felt out of my depth, that I was barely treading water, merely bullshitting my way through it. Bullshitting is not without merit – and I will return to this later – but it may well be a better idea to start elsewhere. Community groups, direct action, mutual support, protest, strikes and other public-facing rights defences should always be on the table, and people like me who focus on more long-term work should support those who are on the streets and picket lines.

My experience has brought me to situations as diverse as protests outside churches and sitting across the table at local policing accountability boards, national healthcare regulators and the United Nations Human Rights Council. This range of experiences has been a massive privilege and a benefit for my knowledge and skills in some ways – I know how not to focus too hard on one thing – but also means my knowledge in any given area isn't going to be as strong as someone who's devoted their life to reforming a single law or resolving a single injustice. Both these approaches are good and needed, but don't just take my word on anything I say here – let this be an introduction to the subject, not the final say. Treat it perhaps like most linguists treat the English dictionary – a useful guidebook on how language can be used, but not the final authority on how the language ought to be used.

Among Us

I've met very few LGBTQ or disability rights activists who came into the work from scholarly study or academic interest. Most of those I've worked with, myself included, got into this work through our own lived experiences or hardships that prompted our interests. Many of us start from necessity and develop our work incrementally until we are genuinely good at something.

It's good to know what you're talking about, but it's not something you ever definitively arrive at one day. I've never talked to an activist about imposter syndrome who hasn't said they've experienced it in heaps – that worry that you're lucking your way into, or not deserving of, access to spaces or recognition. I'm raising this now because it's perfectly natural to feel out of your depth or daunted about human rights, and I argue that in moderation it can be a very good thing indeed. The fact that I'm being trusted by a publisher to write a book about this is very encouraging but also very anxiety-inducing – imposter syndrome loves finding a new arena for worry. I've never written a book before, and to be honest, I'm not sure what success would look like. Is this trust warranted, or is it only being offered because my cat happened to gain popularity online? Hopefully both, because the second definitely plays a role.

As you delve into something you're interested in, you'll inevitably learn a lot about it and develop your skills. Jumping into human rights resources and learning the language – and then just running headfirst into an important issue – can be tempting but risky. If you're working on something with limited representation either locally or more widely, mistakes early can have long-lasting effects, especially with others you have hope of working with. Alienating potential colleagues, appearing crassly arrogant and rude, or simply being unprepared and blundering something important are all things many of us do without meaning to, in all aspects of life.

I'm guilty of this, without a doubt. I have very embarrassing memories from when I was inexperienced in human rights work, meeting with other activists and assuming we had a similar level of knowledge. They were unquestionably more knowledgeable and more skilled than I was, and my presence there was not helpful. I was a teenager, yes, but I burned some bridges that took years to rebuild, and I regret that. I've many examples of these sorts of naïve missteps, and if you're new to human rights, you likely will too, especially if there isn't a skilled, established organisation you can work within.

This is especially important to remember if you're supporting people individually, learning about their specific personal circumstances and helping them out of it. Over-committing and over-promising are attractive but common follies for those in our field, because many of us are very passionate about what we do, and ultimately hopeful that things *will* get better soon. Your timeline and theirs are unlikely to match up, and underdelivering can make them less likely to ask for support in future. Things will hopefully get better in many ways, but if you're urgently needing help in the here and now, 'in the future' may as well be 'never'.

Underdelivering is a huge problem in many areas of human rights work where support for individuals or small groups is provided. Many areas of our work and advocacy are chronically underfunded and are understaffed and overly stretched as a result. As the world around an organisation changes – the COVID-19 pandemic leading to many more individuals needing support, for example – these traps become harder to avoid. Is it better to conserve your energy and do less than you are capable of during normal times so that you have reserves to cope in more challenging unusual times, or to go flat out and hope that more difficult times don't present themselves? There are in-betweens of course, but this thought plagues many of us.

However, the most common scenario I've discussed with other human rights workers is when they worry about being the imposter, lucking their way into a space by having connections or knowing the lingo, while in reality they are the most knowledgeable person in the room. If you're working in areas of thematic rights, like disability rights, women's rights, refugee rights or LGBTQ rights, this is astoundingly common, at least when you're working with people who aren't as focused on the topic as you are. Of course, this isn't something that only affects human rights workers, but there are often high expectations of knowledge and skill on those providing advocacy and expertise in this field, so it may be more common here than elsewhere. The level of knowledge you will need for any given scenario will, of course, vary but having a year of careful learning about LGBTQ rights under your belt is usually more than almost everyone else you will work with outside the specific circle of LGBTQ rights defenders.

Realising this can be a huge relief, especially if you're talking with governments, leaders or others who make important decisions about your society. If you know more than the basics, and especially if you have lived experience of the topics you're discussing, you'll likely be the most knowledgeable person in any given space. Perhaps exposure to online communities can dilute this understanding because we often mix with those of similar interests and experiences online, meaning we appear to ourselves as less knowledgeable than others. However, in this case we're comparing ourselves to others well above the baseline level of knowledge, potentially even with bona fide experts in their field, so worrying you're unfit to talk about disability rights to your local parliamentary representative may be being a bit too careful. In my experience, many activists who are kept away from the tables of decision makers are more knowledgeable and skilled than those with constant access, often because it's not just knowledge and skill that determine who is granted access and who is excluded. If you've got this far, hopefully it's not a shock to suggest that discrimination and hostility are common experiences against marginalised human rights workers, which shamefully keeps underrepresented activists away from decision makers and on a global scale hinders activists from the Global South.

However, when imposter syndrome doesn't take over everything, and as long as it's not written off where it might be relevant, it's useful for helping ensure your feet are planted to the ground and your ego kept in check. A lot of human rights defenders I've talked with over the years, and myself included, have suffered from a devastating lack of confidence about our own skills, or worry that the knowledge we have is far too niche or far too specialised to be useful. My niche is the intersection between disability rights, gender and sexual orientation. Sure, it's not got its own agency at the UN, but there is abundant work to be done. In a world of many billions of people but zero countries with a clean bill of health on human rights, it's almost guaranteed you'll have work to do.

TIME TOO GET HIGH

CHAPTER SIX

Using What You Know

If you want to get started with human rights work, you may find yourself worried about what you could add. The expectations that many people come into this field with are that they need to be knowledgeable about the law at a high level, or be able to crunch through hefty reports and dense academic writing. If you're applying for a job in a human rights law firm, sure, that may be the case, but the vast majority of human rights workers are not lawyers or legal experts. Regardless of your age and experience, you very likely have skills that are useful for the progression of human rights work. This is why I always try to frame human rights work as much broader than the current societal perceptions of what it involves, because as I outlined in earlier chapters, human rights work is everything from legal battles to education, music and art to care work, fundraising to online organising.

Whether you're an artist, an educator or someone with an understanding of how to build an audience online, your skills

79

are important in moving human rights efforts around the world forward. When I made my first moves into trans community organising in 2013, my skills were mostly around building online communities and growing audiences, and some basic knowledge about LGBTQ rights topics like healthcare and marriage equality. Hardly a law degree – after all, I just wanted to spend time with other people like me. The others I met through starting that small trans youth meetup brought their own skills and know-how, from graphic design to knowledge about local event spaces and festivals. Others contributed their time to help run the events physically, keeping people safe and cleaning up afterwards. We all met up with a very basic understanding of what we wanted to do, and limited ability to do it individually, but together it worked quite well. Over time, several of us developed into highly specialised international human rights activists, and others preferred to work in their local communities, helping young people or running friendly events. Still others used their time in activism to develop their skills more broadly and use their resultant graphic design or campaigning talent to earn a living to fund their volunteering. All of these paths are equally legitimate and, crucially, equally necessary. Local organising and community support will likely be needed for the rest of our lives at the very least, and no matter how the world changes around us, people will seek out those who understand their problems. Your country's exit from the European Union, or the collapse of the United Nations human rights mechanisms, is unlikely to make your local human rights challenges any less pressing, so no matter what your path in this field, respect and support for your local organisers and workers is important.

Besides, knowing everything and doing everything isn't feasible unless you're immune to exhaustion and very wealthy, in which case you live in a very different world from most of us, but it also makes your efforts more vulnerable to drift or collapse should you need to step away. Movements and communities organised collectively are usually more challenging to manage and to establish consensus within, but they are often more resilient to hardship as a result. I've been a keystone of several projects I've been a part of during my time in activism work because of how new and unprecedented it was in Northern Ireland at the time, but that is not a position I recommend anyone to be in, if at all possible, because it's a lot of pressure for little outcome. Instead, wherever feasible, each person contributing what they can comfortably deliver, and learning from the others as the work progresses, will more often lead to sustainable and resilient movements. Of course, it is never this simple, and my activism to this day involves an uncomfortable balance of both of these approaches, because we're still too young and too underfunded.

My point here is that if you want to help your local LGBTQ group or join a disability advocacy movement, campaign for the end of a war your country is involved in, or demand your government accepts climate refugees, no matter what your cause is, there will be a place where you can help. Cooking and catering, medical and care support, cleaning and administrative work, tech support and communications coordination, childcare and transport, all of these are important roles for many human rights movements, they're just less discussed. Just like everything else in society, protest and civil rights movements depend on a huge amount of relatively unseen, back-room work, and one of my hopes is that these roles become more celebrated for their importance.

Of course, you may need to build up your knowledge if you want to use your skills with nuance and develop a range of tactics. Having a goal – to lead a campaign, to design a logo which makes a movement successful via its recognisability, to drive a bus to Pride every year for your local community group – can be a useful impetus to build that skill – public speaking, graphic design, driving – and can make learning much more enjoyable. I've dived into many new skills and topics through interest spurred via my activism, and they've helped me become a better activist as a result. Regardless, whatever you walk into this field with will be enough for you to get started. In particular, if you hope to fight for the rights of a marginalised group of which you're a member, you possess something very valuable indeed – your lived experience.

Nothing about us without us

Having been a saying in Eastern Europe for centuries, the phrase 'Nothing about us without us' originated in its English form in disability rights advocacy during the 1990s, used by disabled people demanding the same right to make decisions about their own lives as nondisabled people enjoy.[1] It simply demands that disabled people be the deciders of their own fate, that they have a meaningful say in their life course like everyone else does. In the context of human rights work, it is also understood to mean the demand that disabled people be represented and involved in their own rights movements at every level, to lead the calls for change and to shape their own community. The phrase has been adopted by many other movements of marginalised groups, including LGBTQ organisations, to demand similar community leadership and representation.

When you have lived your life as part of a marginalised or minority community, you have lived experience of that community. This doesn't mean you have a profound understanding of what your community needs or should demand, but rather that you know personally, from first-hand experience, what being a member of that community is like. Although many attempts at approximating lived experience have been made – by allies to LGBTQ people canvassing opinions and using those to decide what to campaign on, for example – it is a type of knowledge that's impossible to replicate. As an example, a nondisabled person could study disability rights for years and develop a significant understanding, but they would likely still lack the intuition on how their work translates to the real-life experiences of those they advocate for. Having direct, often painful experiences of social and legal discrimination, hardship and exclusion shapes our priorities, and moulds what we perceive as reasonable methods for activism and acceptable outcomes from that work.

Human rights movements are moving, some faster than others, to an expectation that they be led by those with lived experience of what they advocate for. This isn't possible in every circumstance – for example, where those advocated for are stripped of legal rights or liberty which prevents them from self-advocacy, such as people currently imprisoned or under mental health guardianship law – but is a useful goal in most areas of human rights work. The movement from which 'Nothing about us without us' germinated is perhaps one of the more reluctant sectors to change, with the lack of representation of disabled people still being a big issue in many disability rights organisations across the world.

This brings us to one of the issues many marginalised activists encounter when demanding their community voices be heard: their very marginalisation results in them being taken less seriously or treated as less deserving. After all, if someone you don't respect needs something from you, you're less likely to provide it for them if they ask you directly than if someone you *do* respect does it on their behalf. This leads to a problem: how do you ask people without lived experience to give up power to your community when your community isn't taken as seriously, or isn't seen as equally capable of acting in its own best interests?

What lived experience means will differ from person to person, and from community to community. In groups where society assigns you membership at birth – for example, race and ethnicity, nationality, gender (for most people) – your lived experience will shape your childhood, adolescence and adult life continuously, and you may establish strong ties to your community early in life. For those who are categorised into marginalised communities in adolescence or adulthood – for example, most LGBTQ people and people whose disabilities are acquired or become noticed later in life – your lived experience may change as you are perceived differently or may 'begin' in adulthood. A trans person is likely to experience life differently than a cis (non-trans) person as they grow up, but their lived experiences will change substantially if they come out as an adolescent or adult, and they suddenly have to navigate a very different, more hostile world. They're less likely to have established connections to other trans people, and as a result their priorities and approaches in activism may be less tied to intergenerational precedent and tradition. Who is and who isn't considered part of a community varies too, and this affects who is accepted as a leader or activist with lived experience and who is not.

Lived experience is not a golden key to successful activism – you are likely to encounter discrimination as a result – and isn't a get-out-of-criticism-free card either – there are anti-rights grifters in every community who profit from presenting themselves as a token 'good minority' for conservatives – but is an invaluable bank of knowledge should you wish to use it. Overall, activists with lived experience enjoy better trust with the communities they advocate for, and improved access to those communities as a whole, which can help keep their work relevant and up-to-date with emerging trends and developments which affect them. They're also more likely to experience these developments themselves, which can help them understand their urgency and importance should things change for the worse. This personal connection can get... rough, though.

Living with those experiences

Advocating for your own community's rights means you're likely to be in the loop with new developments and risks, which can help your work for sure, but it can also hurt your heart. Personally, the rise of anti-trans hostility and organising in the UK over the past few years has ridden roughshod over my mental health. The progress which we had achieved – moderate but meaningful changes in education, healthcare and civil society to make things better for trans people of all ages – were increasingly lambasted in the press, either as dangerous to children, or as the erasure of women in politics and sport, or as the latest moral panic. British tabloids, and the media as a whole, took the lessons they learned from their decades of homophobic sensationalism and turned to focus on this new target. Trans people are a tiny minority of the population, but our human rights issues have been reframed as a new threat – depending on who you ask – to women's rights, children's protections, 'common sense' or even Western society and culture, poised to unravel decades of progress in health, education and political rights for other groups. This tactic was adopted from its true savants, conservatives in the US, but used to greater success in the UK.[2] We saw progress in many of our human rights efforts grind to a halt, governments and regulators poisoned by doubts seeded by these new anti-trans actors, and rollbacks have slowly started to follow. Many activists I worked beside in years past have had to step down to protect their own well-being, and I don't fault them for it, because trans rights activism in much of the UK is now much harder than it was just a handful of years ago, with much higher personal risks to activists and their safety.

Being a 'professional' trans person, or disabled person, or indigenous person, or refugee, means you don't get a day off from discrimination or hostility, and turning off at the 'end' of the workday can be difficult. I think this is why high-level human rights work is attractive for many of us, because it allows some separation from our workday and the rest of our lives. Working locally or nationally against something which affects your life negatively every day is difficult. For example, in the lead-up to Ireland's 2015 marriage equality referendum, many activists' health suffered as they spent their days advocating against hateful and careless hostility from the No campaign, and then spent their nights seeing the very same on television and on posters strapped to streetlights outside their windows. Activists today fighting against anti-trans movements around the world still find themselves surrounded by hostility in the press and in their local societies, and this can be very hard to live with for long periods. The constancy of hostility and discrimination is experienced by many, many marginalised groups, as many of us are one tabloid moral panic away from all-encompassing hatred online and in the press. Sometimes, stepping away feels very attractive indeed.

If I had any advice, it would be to step away when you need to, if at all you can. My biggest regret over the past years of activism is not taking enough time off, and not taking care of my health as a result. Although I took weekends off where I could, the separation of work and the rest of my life was hard to maintain, and my social media circles and hobbies didn't meaningfully separate themselves from work to bring much meaningful rest. The phrase 'if you love your work, you'll never work a day in your life' is a lie, especially where the work you're trying to accomplish helps your life and the lives of your community to be better in the future. Burnout is hard to recover from when you're surrounded by its instigator every day, so proactively spending time to rest and do things you enjoy with people you love is wise. I wish I'd learned earlier, and I wish I would follow my own advice more today.

CHAPTER SEVEN

Success Stories

I've always found it interesting how dissimilar I and the human rights activists I know are as people compared with much of the work we create. Reading through human rights toolkits, resources and literature, it's easy to miss the underlying drive for the work we do, which I believe is strongly emotional. Perhaps this is because we are expected to work alongside business, legal and international diplomatic circles where politeness, 'proper' language and calm are expected, but the majority of human rights activists I've worked with are fiery and passionate individuals. They work juggling these expectations as required, but don't get any less emotional as people. For many human rights defenders, to be at the tables where decisions are made, expectations on behaviour need to be met or they risk expulsion. This has been part of the reason behind the professionalisation of human rights organisations I discussed in earlier chapters, but I'm hopeful that the undying emotions in many activists will help this change in future.

I believe much of human rights work and activism is deeply emotional, motivated by love and care for others. This can seem to some as soppy and self-aggrandising, which, in excess, it might be, but I consider most activism for justice and progress to be much closer to care work than capitalist business, nearer peace than war. After all, if you are advocating for people in your community to have better, happier lives tomorrow, it surely must be motivated by love and care for others to some degree, even if you stand to benefit also. This may be especially the case where people with lived experience are striving for justice, keen that others like them avoid the hardship they suffered themselves.

I hope this feels as natural to you as it does to me, but I think this side of our work is too often hidden by the rituals of properness we're often expected to perform. The rise of social movements coordinated through social media, growing until they find themselves covered by global media outlets, might help to change this. The strength of anti-fascist and social justice movements shows a more emotional, raw and honest form of human rights activism than the comparatively intimidating halls of the UN to countless millions. Indigenous rights movements and the contemporary Black Lives Matter movement have been some of the most continuous and strongest challenges to state oppression in recent history, and although often using those 'high-level' professional human rights mechanisms, they gain coverage, and as a result popularity, from disruptive direct action. Oil pipeline blockades, mass protests and immediate reactions to human rights violations – police murders, environmental devastation and countless more – have got their causes in the newspapers. Those newspapers have often been far from complimentary about the tactics used, but they have helped ensure these movements' longevity and legacy by making potential supporters and allies aware.

Telling a story

Using the media to your advantage as a human rights defender isn't an easy task, but I've found some success doing so, having learned from both LGBTQ leaders from previous decades and from these other contemporary movements I've discussed. Basic media training is useful – knowing what you want to say before you say it will get you out of a lot of pitfalls, as will being able to deal with journalists who have less than innocent motives – but beyond this, storytelling is the skill I value the most. Storytelling – being able to tell a relatable, truthful and powerful story about something – is a wonderful thing to be able to do, and holds deep importance in many societies around the world, including my own here in the Irish tradition. Human rights is often associated with partisan politics, especially when it relates to issues society categorises as moral, philosophical or spiritual, and this can lead to certain groups raising their guard upon its mention. Talking about human rights issues in academic or strictly logical ways has its place – educating those already on board with your cause, talking with decision-makers and governments and planning internally – but reaching those outside your existing supporter base is difficult when you stick to these methods.

Despite all your efforts, it's likely that for any given human rights issue, there will always be a group of individuals who will never support your cause. It's important not to ignore these groups – monitoring their organising is useful so you can better address their attempts to frustrate or sabotage your work – but tailoring your messaging to them is often unwise too. Focusing on your ardent opponents focuses you to over-moderate your messaging, removing or cloaking anything that will spook them, and hollowing out what you're working towards. Perhaps the most widespread example of this is in partisan politics itself, where countless left-wing political parties have succumbed to neoliberalism, centrism and an abandonment of leftist values in recent decades to appeal to those in the right wing, and to beg favour from media and business groups. The gutting of Labour Party values in the UK through Tony Blair's New Labour programme is one of the best-known examples of this and helped normalise the expectation that rejection of leftist politics was vital for any political campaign to be seen as credible.[1]

Instead, it's usually wise to focus your messaging on those who vaguely support you (or who support issues close to what you're advocating for), those who are indifferent and those who are only vaguely opposing your work. This tactic has worked wonders for countless right-wing political campaigns in the 2010s, which onboarded potential new supporters through targeting the politically apathetic and centre-right while simultaneously building zealotry through radicalisation of their pre-existing supporter base. The rise of right-wing extremism across the world during this time, from Britain to Brazil, Hungary to the US, benefited enormously from these tactics. By targeting those susceptible to their messaging – in many cases, to those hurt by the recent abandonment of leftist values by previous governments, ironically – while ensuring their opponents' work was stymied with responses to the moral panics and manufactured crises they invented, these groups saw outstanding success. They told stories of 'normal people' hurt by 'leftist' and 'social justice' causes, and repeated ad infinitum the hypothetical dangers of what people like us were supposedly working in the name of.

There's a big difference between human rights defenders like us and those who build their life around opposing us, though. As proven time and time again via electoral integrity and fact-checking methods in recent years across multiple countries, the stories that these antagonising groups tell are all too often simply fabricated. Instead of giving exposure to real people in their own communities suffering from an injustice they want to eradicate, their messaging is often based in hypothetical extremes, twisted beyond reality or even completely falsified. Partially because of the attempts of groups like these, and because of human rights violations as a whole, activists sadly have no shortage of stories to tell, and no imperative to spice these up with misrepresentation and lying. Many of the greatest human rights achievements in recent history – the overturning of apartheid in South Africa, the fall of far-right military dictatorships in South America and, closer to my home, the decriminalisation of homosexuality in Ireland – were all progressed through the telling of human stories by those demanding change. By telling true stories of human suffering at the hands of state oppression, the inherent empathy they invoke grabs most people's interests, opens them up to listen and ultimately brings them on board.

This can, to a degree, be demonstrated in a more general way through the changes in societal attitudes towards LGBTQ people across many societies in recent years. Queer people coming out introduces people in their life to an understanding of their human rights issues, making those people less likely to be hostile to others, which slowly improves society's response to queer issues. This leads to more people coming out, more people having interpersonal connections to LGBTQ rights and more support in general. This continues to snowball, and over decades support for LGBTQ rights changes from a small minority of personally connected people to an expectation of polite society. In these examples, the stories of people's friends and families bring them on board, protect them from radicalisation into hateful ideas and enable societal progress in a small way. Stories from LGBTQ people themselves and those of their families have different responses in different groups, but both can be used to great effect to reach those traditionally unwelcoming of activist and human rights messages, alleviate many of their concerns and build an expectation that support is the decent, human thing to provide.

We can use this approach in an organised way to progress human rights efforts much more quickly and successfully. When advocating for a certain cause – for example, access to affirming healthcare for trans young people – providing trans young people with the ability to tell their stories, explain how issues affect them and outline how reasonable their needs are helps to reach all groups but the most ardent opposition. In this case, it's likely wise to also provide for parents and guardians to tell their stories in addition, to access those who might discount young people's testimony but be more likely to listen to other adults, especially those with children. Explaining their needs in a straightforward way, free of academic language and legal discussion, is a useful way of using mass media to achieve what trans young people have been doing individually with their own families for many years, but en masse and with less risk for those involved. Indeed, it also helps spur more of this long-established individualised change, as by showing trans young people others like them in the media, they feel safer and more able to come out themselves. Through the telling of stories of parents and guardians, readers or listeners who are also parents and guardians can empathise, considering the lengths they may go to for their own children and considering what they would do themselves.

Of course, this doesn't work for everyone. In fact, it can be easily weaponised by antagonists, telling rare or even hypothetical stories of the minority of trans young people or carers who advocate against affirming healthcare. The protection of children has been used by countless antagonists to human rights across the decades to argue their points of view about, for example, racial desegregation, the decriminalisation of homosexuality, the provision of sex education and abortion, and refugee rights around the world. 'Think of the children' is invoked to great benefit and great detriment to human rights causes every day, and this should be kept in mind when building a campaign to prevent susceptibility to this form of attack.

Luckily, my own island has two great examples of this in recent years. Ireland's marriage equality referendum in 2015 closely followed by its campaign for gender recognition for trans people focused heavily on storytelling to build support. Despite a well-resourced and adamant opposing No campaign, the stories of the Yes campaign gave the spotlight to same gender couples, their children and their families to tell their story about what marriage would mean to them. There are many criticisms to be made of the marriage equality campaign, and indeed their hesitancy and conservatism in messaging did indeed alienate a significant chunk of LGBTQ people in Ireland, but their storytelling worked. Representing the experiences of relatable Irish people as they explained in everyday language why marriage was important for them and their families helped the public connect with and take interest in the issue. Almost every Irish person has a family and knows what Irish families are like, and so seeing LGBTQ people as someone who could be in your family is a reliable way to get the public to open up. The use of stories was clever, led to great success and should be learned from by those hoping to achieve similar aims. Similar stories were and are told by trans rights movements in Ireland, describing the pain of the denial of legal recognition, and demonstrating how reasonable their requests were. Ireland, traditionally a very conservative, Catholic country, has seen enormous change in recent years (both for the better and for the worse), but activists' use of storytelling across multiple areas of human rights work has been world class.

llook at all thos beans

Hearts hurting

One of my earliest memories of world events was watching the collapse of the Twin Towers on the small portable television in the kitchen, played on repeat for hours. I remember thinking it was big, but I doubt many people my age expected its response to last for the majority of our lives, both abroad in endless conflict and at home with security apparatus and domestic surveillance. The end of the war in Afghanistan in 2021 saw millions of adults live the first days of their lives without the war being a part of it, yet their suffering continues with famine emerging from international sanctions and restrictions on food imports imposed on them from the same powers that terrorised them for decades. What now?

We're all used to the world ending. Growing up with apocalyptic disaster movies – *The Day After Tomorrow* being my childhood favourite, despite the dodgy pirated DVD we had – showed us countless different ways we could come to our demise as a global society and a species. As it turned out, our lessons about acid rain in primary school were the least of our problems, as the past decade of increasingly extreme weather events have shown us mere glimpses of climate change's unfolding grand horrors.

We now have wealth disparities in many nations not seen in a century, a global pandemic that's killed millions and permanently injured tens of millions, and intellectual property controls restricting who can manufacture vaccines, condemning hundreds of millions of people in the Global South to needless exposure and illness, all to protect profits in the Global North. This understandably leads many people to apathy, despair and hopelessness.

Many activists I've talked to over the years of my own work have described how hard it is to see past the all-encompassing dread that surrounds us a lot of the time. Although it is possible to separate ourselves from the horrors of the world – to various degrees from person to person, of course – human rights work inevitably involves suffering, pain, despair and hopelessness in some way or another. I've seen colleagues step away from their work after years of targeted harassment in the press, others quit due to being traumatised by what they've been exposed to, and more still resign because they developed chronic health issues from the stress of their work.

This isn't unlike what others experience in life – carers, doctors, therapists, parents and plenty others do too – but the frameworks for supporting human rights workers are usually much less developed than in other roles, and combined with more hostile working environments, increasingly many of us burn out or get hurt. Sometimes it's the work itself, and sometimes it's something else entirely.

Bombs and bullets

I found myself having to step away from work in the middle of 2019, when my friend Lyra McKee was shot and killed in her adopted city of Derry in the northwest of Northern Ireland. Lyra and I had spent many hours together driving around Northern Ireland visiting locations she wanted to visit as part of her investigatory work aimed at uncovering injustices committed during our country's recent violent past. She joked about how one day she'd end up getting shot by digging up unwelcome answers to shady questions, but that joke has soured since. She was intensely interested in people, and her joy talking about her own fascinations seemed only matched when she was listening to friends describing theirs. Lyra was an investigative journalist, keen to uncover truths so that peace could flourish through justice. She was a massive inspiration and a key driving force behind much of what I've done, egging me on to launch the biggest things I've tried so far, and indeed asking me regularly about when I'd write this book. We said we loved each other on a snowy night on the mountain road back into Belfast. Her loss is indescribable.

The New IRA, a paramilitary group rejected by most in this part of the world, accepted responsibility for her murder, and the world's press repeated her name for several days. I became deeply thankful for Irish Catholic traditions around death, spending time with the deceased in person and retelling stories, jokes, wishes. Someone who had given so much hope to me, a person I shared so much mutual trust and learning with, was suddenly gone. We were ceasefire babies, born within a couple of years of each other, promised by older generations the peace they had worked towards for decades. Lyra's murder was devastating to those who knew her, especially her family and friends, but I noticed a specific pain in those of us around her age. We had all known about other younger people's lives being taken in paramilitary violence in recent years, but the personal loss of someone so dear to us vaporised our ideas of what peace meant, and some of us have seen our viewpoints shift profoundly since, myself included.

Radicalisation for the better, disrobed of apathy through trauma. Personally, I think recovering from her loss is unlikely right now, but the anger and fury towards her murderers that I've fought with has been enlightening as to how I might deal with devastation in future.

'Here's to better times ahead, and saying goodbye to bombs and bullets once and for all.' One of Lyra's tweets from a few months before her death, celebrating her move to her new city of Derry with the love of her life.

I'm a changed person since Lyra's murder, less happy and more cynical, unable to work like I used to, but I've also been forced to take better care of myself and others, and I've become less afraid of speaking candidly about my beliefs. In fact, it's forced me to find those beliefs.

Knowing what you really want

Thinking back to an earlier chapter when I asked you as a reader what you might like to see in a better world, it's time to think about what that really means. Even if you know what you want to see in the world and earnestly believe in its importance, it can be difficult to establish how best to move towards those goals. Although much of this difficulty arises because societal problems are complicated, interdependent and entrenched over decades, the actions needed to resolve them require us to examine what we believe, politically and socially, and to communicate that to others. Success for human rights defenders involves a handing over of power and autonomy to those who are currently marginalised, but by definition, it also involves the removal of power from those who currently wield it.

Let's take an example. A better society to you may be one where everyone has a roof over their head and where homelessness is no longer a concern. There are many ways to achieve this – subsidising landlords to top up the rent of poorer tenants, setting upper limits on rent costs, seizing empty buildings and land to create social housing, paying everyone a basic income to cover living expenses, or guaranteeing everyone a home of their own – but which is the most just? Some of these options, like universal basic income or expanding housing benefits and landlord subsidies, expand current social safety nets but don't challenge the underlying structures that have led to current housing crises – namely that property is treated like any other market commodity and exploited for profit. Others, like rent caps, abandoned property seizures and social housing programmes, challenge private renting and home ownership as the only options available but still legitimise private landlording. Others, like guaranteeing a home to everyone through social housing, may require private landlords to become a thing of the past.

Each of these options attempts to end homelessness, at least on the surface. Moreover, each of these solutions is campaigned for by different housing rights advocates, but they derive from completely different underlying political motivations. Should housing be a right, or should *safe and stable* housing be? If a landlord can deny you housing because of who you are, or because you're on benefits, is your right to housing infringed upon? Can a landlord kick you out just so they can increase the rent as your area gets gentrified? Which do you think would solve a housing crisis for generations, not for years, and which do you want to see attempted?

An example on a thematic human rights topic could be the right for disabled people to make their own decisions about their lives. In the 2020s, many disabled people – particularly those with learning disabilities, developmental disabilities and some mental health problems – are prevented from choosing where, how and with whom they live through guardianship, mental capacity and mental health law. The UN Convention on the Rights of Persons with Disabilities – which most countries have ratified – already prohibits this, guaranteeing all disabled people rights to make their own decisions, in every situation. No country in the world reaches this standard, and exceedingly few have made substantial progress towards this goal. For all disabled people to have decision-making rights on par with nondisabled people, options suggested by activists have included everything from allowing individuals to choose their own conservators or co-decision-makers, ensuring judicial oversight to limit what decisions others get to make about a disabled person, to abolishing forced detention and forced treatment altogether, closing inpatient mental health and learning disability facilities and requiring everyone to be included in the community. Like the housing example above, these solutions span a wide variety of political beliefs, and challenge existing power dynamics to different degrees. Which are easily achieved progress, and which are meaningful and substantial improvements for disability rights? Which, if any, provide equality?

These spectra of proposed solutions exist in every area of human rights and politics without exception. From tackling climate change (encouraging electric vehicles, implementing carbon taxes to banning cars, nationalising energy, and converting to renewables) to improving workplace rights (quotas for marginalised workers, the right to unions and collective bargaining to mandatory co-operative company structures) to the addressing of countless other topics, there are many approaches activists call for. What we consider our goals and what we consider unacceptable determines the type of human rights work we end up doing, but it also places us on a political spectrum that many of us try to avoid when at all possible. For better or worse, human rights work and most forms of social activism are inherently political, and the designation of certain rights issues – workplace unionisation, housing rights, healthcare rights – as highly political is itself a political tool to moderate their progress.

If you want to dip your toe into human rights work, you may not yet understand in great detail how you might achieve your goals, but you most likely do have an idea of what a better world looks like to you. I've found it very useful to consider this type of spectrum when thinking about what you want to achieve in your activism, because thinking about the possibilities – however extreme some of they may appear at first – can help clarify in your head what fits best with your overarching worldview. Human rights work will likely change your worldview somewhat as you get involved, learn more about the topic, hear stories from activists and leaders, and begin to establish your own political and philosophical framework for what kind of work you want to do.

Knowing what you want is good, but knowing what needs to happen for you to succeed makes you more able to communicate with others, both to those you work alongside and to those you hope to bring on board as supporters and allies. It also reveals your opposition.

I'm a socialist, and most activists I've worked alongside are leftists also. Personally, this seems natural, because human rights based on mutual respect, equality, kindness and love for others are much more accessible when everyone – no matter their background or standing in society – has housing, quality healthcare, support and respect at work, and protection from the hardships of poverty. These baselines of social protection allow people to spend more time with those they love, be creative and expressive and, just as importantly, rest. As the past decades have shown, these basic comforts are much less accessible under right-wing governments, and they suffer at the hands of right-wing campaigns. The tools of successful right-wing leaders, governments and pundits overwhelmingly rely on the weaponisation of human rights in their messaging, from decrying social security systems and public spending, stirring moral panics over the human rights of marginalised people potentially trampling on those of the majority, and the use of nationalism and militarism to stoke tension and conflict.

Much of this is, ultimately, led by business interests. Referring again to Naomi Klein's work in *The Shock Doctrine*, everything from the installation of right-wing governments around the world by the US to the hollowing out of European democratic structures by privatisation and austerity measures has raked in endless billions for those with the deepest pockets.[2] The accumulation and concentration of extreme wealth into fewer and fewer hands during the COVID-19 pandemic represents merely an acceleration of what has been well underway in most of the world for decades – the prioritisation of profit over human lives.

Regardless of where your interest in human rights defence points you, it's likely you will be presented with this perverse prioritisation eventually. Anti-war activists will meet the resistance of the biggest defence contractors in the world. Climate change campaigners will have to fight the petrochemical sector, some of the most well-funded lobbying efforts in human history. LGBTQ community groups will struggle for media exposure among tabloids making healthy profits from every moral panic they fuel, and often against conservative movements funded by groups with no horse in the race but profits still to be made. In every case I have ever encountered, those fighting for human life and dignity over business interests will see their financial and institutional resources outmatched. This doesn't make progress for human rights defenders impossible or even unlikely, but it's a rigged game.

pelase do not disturb ,my work

CHAPTER EIGHT

Keeping a Roof Over Your Head

As may have become obvious by now, human rights work and activism are never going to be the most glamorous or the most lucrative work you'll find. For many activists, financial security takes a long time to establish, and many of us will have to rely on other sources of income to do the work we love. However, and although this will depend on your own circumstances, there are myriad ways you might find feasible.

For most people – and where the issues aren't immediately life-or-death – human rights work isn't something you have to do full-time. You can set your own timescales for getting started, and gradually ease yourself into these new experiences as you slowly build knowledge and confidence. Given the nature of much of this work, it's important to pace yourself to make sure your health – physical and mental – and finances are protected as well as possible.

However, if you want to devote a substantial amount of time and effort to human rights work, there are a few things to consider to make sure your housing and health stay secure as you get started. Throughout my experience of being a human rights activist since 2013, I have had to support myself financially, but have only had a formal salary for one of those eight years. For most of that time I was on a very low income, below what out-of-work benefits would have provided, but in recent years this has improved, mostly because my audience online grew substantially. As I write this book, I don't have a salary anymore, and the COVID-19 pandemic decimated my income, so I'm still very familiar with financial uncertainty. It's not news to anyone in human rights circles that our work often comes with stress and poor pay, but much of my work has involved the establishment of community spaces and resources that simply didn't exist before, meaning that drawing down a salary was not even remotely possible.

So, how do you keep a roof over your head when you're getting started in all of this? The answer will depend on where you are in the world, the laws you have to follow, how much you're able to work, whether you have children or a family to support, and whether you have other costs I could never foresee. However, many of the individuals I've worked alongside over the past few years have entered this work in a similar way to myself, meaning they couldn't rely on a salary to pay the rent and fill the refrigerator. Human rights jobs often come with short contracts, long hours and difficult conditions, and resources fluctuate with political changes, public spending and social attitudes. With decreased funding for many groups, the gig economy has not passed human rights work by.

If you happen to have the qualifications or experience needed to make a successful application for a paid position at a human rights organisation, this is likely to be the most stable way you can get started. However, unless you happen to drop into a mid- or high-level position, a difficult and inaccessible prospect for many marginalised activists, you are likely to be limited in the work you're able to do in formal employment. In many established advocacy and human rights organisations, employees and activists lower on the corporate tree are much less likely to be able to influence the broader direction of the organisation, especially its motivations and goals. However, if you have substantial specialised skills, you may be able to influence its wider activity with those – for example, in campaigning or communications. If you're the most knowledgeable person in an organisation about a certain issue, this can come with increased access and influence.

One point to note, however, is that human rights work can't flourish without support. Although designing campaigns, lobbying governments and representing your work in the media are often what we think of when we imagine human rights work, the administrative, technical, caring and cleaning work needed to make these organisations run is easily as important. If you want to support a human rights movement or organisation with this sort of work – cleaning, accounting, childcare, counselling, transport and logistics, technical support – or if you are content to do it while working towards more public-facing activity, you are still supporting human rights work.

If you have the qualifications and can feasibly acquire a paid position, you are in a relatively rare and privileged position compared to most activists, and you should consider this when making a decision on how to get started. Though only achieved after years of work, I have held (mostly unpaid) higher-level positions before and have enjoyed their privileges, and I am taking that into consideration when writing this chapter. Experiencing these benefits can easily blinker your ideas about employment and financial stability in human rights work, so it's important to look back to the barriers that remain to getting started with this work.

Other paths that may be open to you include gradually starting human rights work on top of salaried work you already do; using a period of time that you're on a student income, out-of-work benefits or disability benefits to develop your human rights skills; or perhaps being or becoming self-employed and raising money in another way as you begin to feel your way into this field. This last approach is the route I took, and it has brought success, and some level of security, but this comes with asterisks attached.

Back to Bilbo

One of the reasons my cat Bilbo has been so central to my human rights work is that his fanbase has made much of that work possible. Through stabilising my income and building my public platform to reach more people, I've been able to gradually build connections within human rights circles and use those to open up new opportunities within the field. Although I try to limit how 'political' Bilbo is online, he's perceived as a loving and welcoming personality, someone who cares about other people no matter who they are. This gels well with human rights work – which as I've discussed I believe is deeply rooted in care and love for others – and he seems to attract those who share my outlook on human rights and social progress. This means his online presence and my work have grown in tandem, and the income his significant following brings in through merchandising has paid the rent while I worked unpaid elsewhere. However, this took years, patience, luck, living in a relatively inexpensive part of the country and a cultural internet savvy developed over more than a decade of being far too online. Accounts like Bilbo's are much more common now – in small part due to his success and reach – and it's a much more crowded market in 2021, so financial security via pet social media accounts may not be the wisest route to take. However, the specific skills, knowledge and interests you've already developed likely have potential to help you get going in your own direction, and there are countless niches in online creation that have public interest yet to be satisfied. Creators of all sorts, and indeed activists of all sorts, have Patreon and other personal fundraising links on their Twitter profiles for this exact reason.

How you decide to make a living will depend on your politics, your beliefs and the context you live in, and there are human rights activists doing everything from driving taxis, selling merchandise and doing sex work to allow them to spend some of the rest of their time progressing human rights for them and their communities. How safe and successful any one activist is in this is heavily influenced by how much they are privileged or marginalised in society, and by how safe their working environments are both within and without human rights work. We are, despite our human rights goals, unfortunately limited in our success by how lucky we are and how we're perceived in the society we wish to change.

Internet lemonade stands

I started making a self-employed income in 2017, when at the request of some of Bilbo's followers I spent a day collaging together hundreds of photos of him into a poster and sending it to a local printshop for production. What followed were several months of clumsy wandering across various online platforms searching for the best way to sell physical things to people across the entire globe. This is surprisingly difficult, even in the age of eBay and Etsy, and selling anything physical often requires the navigation of online payment gateways, web security, content management systems, customs declarations and customer service. A nightmare.

If you don't hold your own stock, there are now myriad platforms for selling goods and services online, allowing you to sell custom merchandise and physical goods all around the world. I started on merchandising platform Bonfire in 2017, with T-shirts themed with trans rights slogans and designs, which allowed me to fund some of the equipment I needed to set up my own small merch operation. If you're an artist or creator, or if you have a renewable source of something you think other people would like, this can be an invaluable way to add to your income or help fund the equipment, furnishings and materials you need to grow your work. Most platforms don't require you to buy in bulk or to warehouse stock, which gets very expensive very quickly and which has been one of the biggest hurdles to merchandising in the past.

Having your own website is a good idea, even if you have successful social media audiences, even if you hate the idea. Having one place to show your work, a place to host files online and an email address with your own web domain name are valuable assets when getting started and growing an audience for your human rights work. In a field like this, where, like many other sectors, the connections you have with others can influence your likelihood of success, appearing like you know what you're talking about can be half the battle. Having readily accessible documentation of your knowledge in one place makes that a lot more feasible.

I now make around 90 per cent of my income from online platforms including my own site, and although I couldn't raise a family on my income, Bilbo and I live comfortably for now. I've turned down more monetisation opportunities than I've accepted, though, because the last thing I want is Bilbo's audience being alienated by commercialisation and missing out on his joy. Growing my human rights work alongside Bilbo's audience is a delicate process, and although Bilbo is no longer the main source of my audience interested in human rights, I still consider it important that his online presence remains as positive and innocent as possible. As a result, my success has been moderate and has largely been limited by choices I've deliberately and pragmatically made, so if you're looking to get rich quick, [extremely BBC Radio reporter voice] other authors are available.

interupting the computer ...important to do

A Twitch in time

As I disgracefully stated earlier in this book, I've been on Twitter so long that my account is old enough to have an account of its own. Growing up on Twitter during the 2010s was a mixed bag – Gamergate, the ascendancy of the far-right and Trumpism, moral panics over trans kids and plenty besides used Twitter as an organising platform and harassment gateway – but it helped me develop a nuanced and skilled savvy in internet culture that makes the kind of human rights work I do a lot easier to discuss online. Although it has rotted my brain and poisoned my humour irreparably, Twitter exposed me to many wonderful individuals who used their platforms to create things they love and communities that follow them. 'Content creators' and 'influencers'. I was a content creator already – because I created content online, understandably enough – but was categorised as an 'influencer' by the UK's Advertising Standards Agency (ASA) when Bilbo's following surpassed 30,000. Now held to their regulation on advertising and promotion, and amused that I, my cat or both of us were considered notable by the ASA, I began researching content creation online and developing some skills to attempt some more technically challenging ideas. I began experimenting on YouTube for a while, a platform I had also grown up with for decades, publishing medium-length videos about human rights and online cultural issues I was interested in, and as COVID-19 restrictions arrived in early 2020, I tried my hand at livestreaming some videogames. It was fun, but it wasn't especially captivating, and my interest waned. Later in the year, I discovered streaming service Twitch via one of my online friends, which despite its age and notoriety, had a culture and energy I was completely unfamiliar with.

Twitch has been the dominant platform for videogame livestreaming for years, and despite challenges from other platforms, remains so to this day. Despite having plenty of experience in online communities elsewhere and having enjoyed both watching and broadcasting live content on YouTube, Twitch showed me a very different side to both internet communities and the things they gather around. The site allows those watching a livestream to send messages in a chat window, displayed prominently alongside the main video player to both the broadcaster and every other viewer, and it's here where I got hooked.

It was in that space, a text chat powered by the same Internet Relay Chat technology that drove chatrooms in the 1990s, where I focused my attention. Many broadcasters have established a form of subculture with their viewers, with linguistic nuances and inside baseball humour that reinforces a sense of being in an in-group, a member of a community. Twitch provides chatters the ability to use emotes – small images, static or animated, in line with text, similar to emojis – to add meaning, context or nuance to their messages, and to communicate a bewildering specificity of emotion in the process.

Most surprising of all was many communities' embrace of emotes depicting Pepe the Frog, whom I had associated only with bad things since his apparent co-option by the alt-right and his creator's disavowal. I had spent weeks blocking hateful messages on Twitter spamming his green face in 2016, and had seen friends be harassed almost to death by those sporting profile pictures of the same. Despite that, here on Twitch, among broadcasters as diverse as teenagers playing The Sims, live podcasts about space and leftist political shows, Pepe was a massive part of chat and the culture as a whole. This left me thinking about where I found myself, and what the platform was really about, but after months of watching and learning, I slowly had a change of heart. Although there were and still are undoubtedly places on Twitch where Pepe still has these connotations, and is used to hateful and harmful ends, the overwhelming majority of users seem to have either reclaimed him back from the far right, or missed his co-option entirely.[1] Users had made their own versions of the froggy character, including cute, shy, excited, giggly and cheering versions, coining 'Peepo' for many of them and iterating upon them again and again for years. Now, almost every large stream I join has Peepos somewhere, and these frogs communicate joy, sadness, excitement, dread and almost every emotion imaginable, but rarely what I had associated him with elsewhere online. In one chat especially – that of leftist broadcaster Hasan Piker (HasanAbi) – I saw human rights and social justice talked about earnestly and with passion alongside Pepes and Peepos. This may seem a strange thing to bring up – bewildering to many, I'm sure, and cataclysmically embarrassing to sincerely write about – but it was a breath of fresh air that helped me rethink what I wanted to do with my human rights work in the years ahead. Human rights are pretty poggers, after all.

I started broadcasting on Twitch in November 2020 and was offered partnership with the platform two months later – an unexpected speedrun to the verified checkmark. I've been broadcasting there regularly since, and in that time, I've come to experience Twitch as the friendliest platform I have ever been a part of, with some of the most wonderful creators to work alongside. Thanks to several hundred supporters, streaming revenue now pays for Bilbo and me to have a roof over our heads with more security than in years gone by, and I'm able to show off things I'm enthusiastic about outside of human rights work too. Finally, my road sign collection has pride of place in my livestream background, and I get paid to wax lyrical about traffic lights – not an outcome I ever expected. This has genuinely been such a relief, and I wish I had done it earlier, because the pressure to always be talking about the horrible things we work against can be exhausting. Although I've been focusing on writing this book in the meantime, I believe Twitch is the best place for me to share human rights education in future, so I intend doing so, starting with the basics, and making it free. This idea and realisation arrived as I was more severely burned out from activism than ever before, quickly losing drive to continue in the field, but the opportunities Twitch has presented to me have reignited my interest intensely. All things being well, by the time you're reading this there will be a regular venue for human rights discussion and learning on Twitch, to everyone, for free. So thank you, Peepo. I'm glad I stuck around.

The online world has changed so much in the past decade, and the COVID-19 pandemic has hammered home its importance in culture and social connection more than anyone could have imagined. Despite the limitations and restrictions of the current plethora of platforms and communities, I think there's hope that new venues and communities that help human rights defenders and connect them with their supporters will flourish in future. In the meantime, there's plenty of paths for human rights outreach and education online that have yet to be explored, and I look forward to seeing how activists and creators – including potentially someone reading this right now – take their first steps along them.

bboy beauty slepe

CHAPTER NINE

The Years Ahead

The 2020s have been rough so far. Much about our world has changed since the start of the COVID-19 pandemic, and it's hard to predict how much of it will recede into memory and how much we'll be experiencing for years to come. The rise of reactionary political figures opposing pandemic restrictions, anti-vaccine conspiracy theorists and junk medicine grifters, and the financial hardships experienced by countless millions since early 2020 have fostered a more hostile, volatile political climate in many parts of the world. Stacked atop millions of needless deaths – many due to government inaction, others due to copyright law preventing poorer countries from accessing vaccines – it's likely this pandemic leaves a traumatic scar across much of society. How this plays out into the rest of the decade and beyond – and what it means for human rights defence and our quality of life in general – is yet to be seen, but there are choppy waters ahead for many.

Unfolding horror

For some, those choppy waters will arrive – if they have not already done so – as increased success for far-right politics, continued prevalence of COVID-19 through anti-medicine conspiracy theories and distrust in vaccinations, and the poverty that often results from long-term economic downturn. As seen in many European countries, including the UK, through proposed policing and secrecy legislation, right-wing governments are accelerating towards authoritarian policy, demonising and badmouthing protest, whistleblowing, workplace strike and human rights activism. Adopting the strategy of invoking moral panic – a timeless classic at this point – the rule of law is presented as being at risk from moralistic and do-gooder activists, lawyers and academics. A return to 'law and order' can mean very different things to different people, and to many union leaders, climate protesters, anti-corruption campaigners and human rights defenders, it can mean restriction of access to state information, erosion of workplace rights through strike prohibitions, and criminalisation of protest and civil disobedience through policing and terrorism legislation. Touching on a previous discussion, these values – workplace rights, climate activism and human rights defence as a whole – are routinely connected to left-wing party politics, mostly because it's useful for their opponents to do so. Human rights are central to meaningful leftist politics in my opinion, but meaningful leftist politics are, more times than not, missing from the larger 'left' parties in most countries around the world. Decades of chipping away at policy and campaign pledges to shift away from traditional ideas of leftism and their USSR associations, and the concurrent move towards neoliberalism, business-friendly policy and centrism have hampered how human rights are discussed across society. Instead of seeing them as society-wide, broad concerns, they are individualised and made personal, detaching them from their social context. The sheer scale of campaigns against moderate socialists like Senator Bernie Sanders in the US and Jeremy Corbyn MP in the UK in the public media show just how far we have to go, with their policies being lambasted as utopian naivety, social justice warrior 'wokeness' and climate do-gooder-ism. Make no mistake – the rejection of left-wing policy in public discussions and in the media is absolutely a major threat to human rights at home in domestic politics and around the globe through foreign policy. Regardless of how 'political' you consider yourself as a current or aspiring human rights defender or activist, your work will be labelled political very quickly if it in any way threatens the current structures of power and profit, so becoming comfortable with this politicisation now can be liberating later.

For others, these choppy waters will arrive quite literally in the form of changing climate – violent weather events like hurricanes, cyclones and typhoons are already on the rise, temperatures continue to trend upwards around the world, and Siberian permafrost is awakening from millennia-long slumber. Although devastating climate change will affect all of us eventually, those least able to mitigate its effects on their own lives have most to lose, with the poor, the marginalised and the young being most at risk. Climate change, like many risks to human rights, will affect almost everyone in the long run, but in the earlier stages further devastates those already under the weight of marginalisation, persecution and poverty.

Yet these unequal effects are exactly the reason why right-wing political leaders are already crying wolf over climate refugees, international trade and global peace – because the suffering and death of the poor, evisceration of national agricultural markets, and conflict sparked by natural disaster are deemed by them acceptable exchange for the preservation of 'our way of life' for us relatively wealthy countries.

Climate change is undoubtedly a human rights catastrophe – not one waiting to happen, because it's already begun, but one which will get worse and worse without action – and it unquestionably affects some more than others. Refugees' rights suffer and famines loom when border crossings are closed after natural disasters in neighbouring countries, impoverished people suffer further when wars spark over resources, and the price of stock market graphs continuing endlessly upwards is merely the rights of a billion children to have a future to live for.

There's certainly cause for concern.

Unfolding hope

There are also reasons to be hopeful. Increasingly, many young people – growing up with constant austerity, an endless war on terror, and their quickly vanishing chances of financial security and fulfilling work – are turning towards the tools of activism, protest and the rejection of right-wing politics as a solution. Support for leftist values and socialist policy has seen rapid and sustained growth in recent years, and the COVID-19 pandemic combined with global protest against police brutality and climate inaction have only increased the pace. Hardship, injustice and suffering can radicalise people in many directions, but for teenagers and young adults, the trend is pointing left. This gives me a lot of hope, and I think the tools that built Bilbo's audience are the very same which have helped this shift towards the left proliferate.

For all the evils that social media and internet communication facilitate, it is undoubtedly a source of hope for the future. Were it not for Twitter and platforms like it, you would not be reading this book, because Bilbo's audience would be just my friends and family, and I never would have been able to connect with human rights defenders and build my knowledge and experience to where it is now. Human rights discussion and campaigning online gets a bad rap – 'Slacktivism' is hardly flattering – but it is demonstrably behind much of the success of movements like Black Lives Matter, whose messages had been ignored by mainstream media for decades. Watching the steady radicalisation of more and more young people online towards these good causes – human rights defence and politics which enable it – has been hugely rewarding personally and a source of sincere hope. It comes from the most baffling of places at times – fans of Minecraft YouTubers teaching each other about workplace protections as an outcome of controversy over merchandise manufacturing, or fundraising efforts for mutual aid projects to help marginalised people during COVID-19 organised by the audience of Twitch streamers – but it translates into the offline world in meaningful ways. Explaining this to those who don't understand it intuitively is difficult because there are years of internet culture, language and etiquette which shape how it works. However, I think that as young people continue to develop the skills to advocate and campaign for what they believe in through online education and community, they will be increasingly seen as serious, bona-fide activists as they translate their skills into offline efforts also.

Leftist and human rights focused creators and broadcasters have existed online for decades at this point, but their success and reach have exploded in the early 2020s, driven by isolated and quarantined young people and young adults seeking information on election campaigns, protest movements and pandemic recovery. As baffling as it sounds, the audiences of Minecraft content creators may now be one of the most successful enabling routes into the baby steps of human rights education for newcomers, and as I've previously mentioned, the largest non-gaming broadcaster on streaming platform Twitch is now Hasan Piker, an unapologetic leftist commentator and educator. It's not unlike how far-right movements enticed online newcomers in with promises of community, friendship and belonging in the 2010s; newcomers to these growing leftist communities often arrive for non-political content, drama, gaming or other entertainment, come back for political discussions, and slowly learn about human rights, political concepts and socialism. As admitted by countless long-term community members in live chat, apathetic viewers become educated, alt-right hate watchers become leftists, and new activists find a voice, all through mostly passive interaction with valuable information and discussion online. Tens of thousands of people now tune in to these creators for overtly and unquestionably leftist discussion which values human rights, social justice and human dignity, with the luckier creators being brought into financial security by their audiences, enabling them to continue and grow their reach.

At the beginning of the 2010s – or even halfway through the decade – much of this would sound ludicrously unlikely amidst the ascendancy of alt-right communities and campaigning at the time, but online culture has shifted substantially during the early 2020s in a reassuringly positive direction. Although the right-wing and anti-vaccine conspiracists still have their audiences online and continue to see success through their grifts, they are now being matched, and increasingly outmatched, by leftist creators and audiences.

Whether this will translate into substantial success for human rights defenders and leftist politics has yet to be seen, but we are now in a position that we've never been in before, and I think there are genuine causes for hope.

In all of this, hope is crucial. Hope for veteran activists can be hard to come by, beaten out by burnout, exhaustion and justified cynicism, but hope for budding activists is crucial, both for building their interest and for developing them into leaders. Despite the enormous challenges that now confront us – continued political hostility, climate disaster and plenty besides – we can't allow desperation to be the only driver of our work. When we extinguish hope for the future or the belief in activism in young people and other potential activists, they fall away, and the marginalised and oppressed people most at risk will inevitably continue to be laboured in their advocacy and campaigning, driven by desperation and suffering. Without communicating hope, even if we have to 'fake it till we make it' for a while, we might just be selling out those most likely to be hurt.

i am nnot hapy ...with your desisions

Ellen and Bilbo, from now on

So, what does the future look like for Bilbo and me? Well, I'm not sure how my health will look like next week never mind next year, so it can be difficult to plan. However, experiences during COVID-19 lockdowns and from my own health problems have showed me I can potentially have more impact through online communities, content creation and discussion than work in person in the offline world. Since discovering the joys of livestreaming, I have an enjoyable and fulfilling way to pay my rent while growing an audience, a valuable combination that's very elusive in other places, and one that's a safe platform for experimentation in human rights education. I'm also approaching my thirties and seeing the value in pacing myself, building security for the future and not working myself to the point of illness as I have been. Although I've made good friends and learned much through international human rights work, the most fruitful route for me might be spreading human rights messaging internationally online, not necessarily working with the United Nations. Realising this has been liberating, and not striving for recognition within the formal structures of human rights mechanisms allows me to focus on what I actually believe and value, while building an audience who want to learn about it.

My work locally in Northern Ireland will continue, however. I'm proud of what we have been able to build with a small group of activists and almost no money, with a unique community centre and support system that others can copy and implement elsewhere. Although Northern Ireland is deeply, deeply flawed, I love it more than most things, and want to continue trying to make it better here for local trans people. What that looks like at the end of the decade, I have no idea, but training up new activists who can achieve what *they* want to do along the way would be a wonderful achievement.

What's next for Bilbo is perhaps a little more certain. For as long as he wants to be here, he'll have a loving home and a doting mother, for what I hope will be for the rest of his years. Bilbo isn't a kitten anymore – he's now seven years old, and his food is labelled '7+ Senior' – and I'm not sure how long he'll be in my life, but I hope we'll be together for many more years.

What happens with Bilbo's Twitter account will depend on both of us. I started taking photos of him as a kitten to document his life and show friends and family, and I'm very happy his account has become as popular as it has. Although I try my best to ensure he's never annoyed or made uncomfortable by my photography as we're enjoying time together, my priority will always be enjoying and treasuring that time together. Bilbo has changed my life for the better in a big way and his audience of fans has ensured we're both able to keep a roof over our head, but if Bilbo grows to not enjoy being online, I'll not hesitate to log out of his account.

Bilbo will always be the good cat boy, whether or not he tweets. Although I have no plans to stop posting his photos online, as we both grow older I will be increasingly considerate of how it might affect us to have so much attention on him, especially as social media platforms change in the future. All things being well, Bilbo will be in a hundred thousand people's lives in a small way, and mine in a big way, for many years to come.

To you

Thank you for getting us to this point. As I left school, I never would have imagined that my life would turn out this way, with a loving cat son helping keep a roof over our heads and helping my human rights work grow to where it is now. To those who helped Bilbo's following grow, thank you, because you've helped so much more than I could ever explain, and you've brought a little bit of joy to people's lives in the process. To my fellow activists and human rights defenders, thank you for sharing your knowledge and skills with me and for the work you do for a better tomorrow. To those who've financially supported me over the years, thank you for giving me room to explore both Bilbo's presence online and my own human rights advocacy and education. Thank you especially to those who pledged to support this book's writing and publication – this was a new, difficult experience, but I hope you found the end result enjoyable.

Thank you to my parents, partners and friends for putting up with this the whole time, and for hopefully putting up with it in the future. To Lyra McKee, thank you for enabling the nonsense that led to this point, and for the fire in your eyes. I will always treasure our friendship for the years we had together, and I love you dearly.

Thank you for reading this book, however you've stumbled across it, and I hope that in future you are – we are – able to look back on some of the challenges and hardships it discusses, not in contemporary anxiety but in reflective memory of a time that came before a better world.

To Bilbo, thank you for being the bboy you are. @thegoodcatboy describes you well.

mimimimimimimimimimimi

Notes

Chapter One: Hello

1 Government Equalities Office, NHS England, 'Government appoints first National Adviser for LGBT Health', press release, Gov.uk, 17 March 2019, www.gov.uk/government/news/government-appoints-first-national-adviser-for-lgbt-health

2 Kathy Maguire, 'Timetable for delivery of Social Inclusion Strategies published', NICVA, 5 October 2020, www.nicva.org/article/timetable-for-delivery-of-social-inclusion-strategies-published

Chapter Two: Ellen the Human

1 Gretchen McCulloch, *Because Internet: Understanding the New Rules of Language*, Penguin Random House, London, 2019, p. 30.

Chapter Three: Bilbo the Cat

1 Claire Sewell and Spencer D. C. Keralis, 'The History & Origin of Cat Memes: From the 18th Century to lolcats; Or, How Cats Have Basically Changed the Internet and the World Furever', *Hyperrhiz: New Media Cultures*, no. 21, 2019, hyperrhiz.io/hyperrhiz21/miscellany/7-cat-memes.html

2 McCulloch, *Because Internet*, pp. 20–50.

3 Hbomberguy, 'DONKEY KONG 64 CHARITY STREAM

ON JANUARY 18TH', YouTube, 15 January 2019, www.you
tube.com/watch?v=WIM-GKRS9Vk

4 XOXO Festival, 'Harry Brewis, Hbomberguy - XOXO Festival
(2019)', YouTube, 9 October 2019, www.youtube.com/watch
?v=lS1k88LzjkQ

5 Patrick Harvie, 'Motion ref. S5M-15504, Online Gamer,
Harry Brewis, Fundraising for Mermaids UK', The Scottish
Parliament, 21 January 2019, www.parliament.scot/chamber
-and-committees/votes-and-motions/votes-and-motions-
search/S5M-15504

6 Kate [@uhh_kate], Twitter, 23 January 2019, twitter.com/uhh
_kate/status/1088107782371528704

7 'bilbo in the news', bilbo, thegoodboy.cat/news

Chapter Four: Cat Twitter

1 peepee the cat [@peepeeplayhouse], Twitter, 19 September
2018, twitter.com/peepeeplayhouse/status/10422906726219366
42?lang=en

2 EllenFromNowOn, 'Cat Twitter', YouTube, 8 November 2019,
www.youtube.com/watch?v=FR6r3QoXbjo

3 StrucciMovies, 'FAKE FRIENDS EPISODE ONE: intro to
parasocial relationships', YouTube, 27 August 2017, www.you
tube.com/watch?v=x3vD_CAYt4g

Chapter Five: Human Rights?

1 Chaka L. Bachmann and Becca Gooch, 'LGBT in Britain:
Trans Report', Stonewall, www.stonewall.org.uk/system/files
/lgbt_in_britain_-_trans_report_final.pdf

2 Naomi Klein, *The Shock Doctrine*, Penguin, 2008, p. 49.

3 David Harvey, *A Brief History of Neoliberalism*, Oxford University Press, 2007, p. 64.

4 Laura Sullivan, 'Plastic Wars: Industry Spent Millions Selling Recycling – To Sell More Plastic', NPR (*All Things Considered*), 31 March 2020, www.npr.org/2020/03/31/822597631/plastic-wars-three-takeaways-from-the-fight-over-the-future-of-plastics

5 Klein, *The Shock Doctrine*, p. 73.

6 David Graeber, *Bullshit Jobs: The Rise of Pointless Work and What We Can Do About It*, Penguin, 2019, p. 145.

7 Nick Martin, 'Liberal Neutrality and Charitable Purposes', *Political Studies*, 60(4): 936–952, 2012, journals.sagepub.com/doi/abs/10.1111/j.1467-9248.2011.00942.x

8 Gerard Quinn, *A Short Guide to the United Nations Convention on the Rights of Persons with Disabilities*, 1 Eur. Y.B. Disability L, 2009, p. 89.

Chapter Six: Using What You Know

1 James I. Clarlton, *Nothing About Us Without Us: Disability Oppression and Empowerment*, University of California Press, 2000, p. 3.

2 Craig McLean, 'The Growth of the Anti-Transgender Movement in the United Kingdom. The Silent Radicalization of the British Electorate', *International Journal of Sociology*, 51(6), 473–482, 2021, www.tandfonline.com/doi/full/10.1080/00207659.2021.1939946

Chapter Seven: Success Stories

1   Alex Niven, 'Blairism failed working-class people', Jacobin, 15 April 2021, www.jacobinmag.com/2021/04/tony-blair-working -class-new-labour-inequality

2   Klein, *The Shock Doctrine*, 2007, p. 281.

Chapter Eight: Keeping a Roof Over Your Head

1   theScore esports, 'The Story of Pepe: The True Face of Twitch', YouTube, 7 August 2021, www.youtube.com/watch?v=mxpbw pU9HAo

Acknowledgements

This book is the outcome of around a decade of knowledge I was graciously taught by those who nurtured my interests. Simon Stewart and Nicola Doran gave me my first opportunities to get involved with local government, and the work of John O'Doherty, Steve Williamson and Cara McCann inspired much of my work in Northern Ireland. Eilionóir Flynn and Maria Ní Fhlatharta sparked my interest in disability law and taught me an endless amount about international law. Alexa Moore, Rain Watt and Naomhán O'Connor helped bring several of the projects I worked on to fruition and they deserve a huge thanks.

My mum Gráinne and dad Jim, my partner Aodhán and my close friends – in particular Toni, Milo and Elaine – were great motivation and excellent proofreaders throughout. They are unfailingly patient during every new project I decide to begin, even when they fail.

I owe a great debt to my dear late friend Lyra McKee, who encouraged me constantly to write this book while she was still with us in the world, and whose memory has brought me encouragement since she left. I hope you like it, Lyra.

Thank you so much to Katy, Anna, DeAndra and the whole team at Unbound for being so helpful, patient and insightful during the process of writing and publishing this book. This is the first time I've done any of this, and I couldn't have done it without their expertise.

Finally, thank you so much to the countless people who've believed in what I do enough to support me before, during and after the process of writing this book, on Unbound, Patreon and Twitch. It is a great privilege to be able to make a living doing what I do, and I thank you all so much.

A Note on the Authors

Ellen Murray is a trans human rights defender who has worked towards LGBT+ human rights in Northern Ireland since 2013. She is Executive Director of TransgenderNI, where she established a long-standing community centre for the trans community in her hometown of Belfast. She was a public appointment to the UK Government's LGBT Advisory Panel, and works as an independent consultant to a variety of international human rights organisations. She is the carer of a beautiful orange cat named Bilbo. Bilbo is a very good bboy.

Bilbo is a good cat bboy from Belfast, Northern Ireland. Born in 2014, he's since grown an audience of fans online who enjoy his round orange face, kind eyes and warm heart. He's brought smiles to hundreds of thousands of people through his tweets, his purring podcast and his way with words. Bilbo lives a comfortable life, with a close circle of cat friends and his favourite dinner served daily. He is quite big and very soft.

The Cat Hall of Fame

Bilbo

Joy

Murphy

Coco

Apollo

Bibou

Pumpkin and Vincent

Unbound is the world's first crowdfunding publisher, established in 2011.

We believe that wonderful things can happen when you clear a path for people who share a passion. That's why we've built a platform that brings together readers and authors to crowdfund books they believe in – and give fresh ideas that don't fit the traditional mould the chance they deserve.

This book is in your hands because readers made it possible. Everyone who pledged their support is listed below. Join them by visiting unbound.com and supporting a book today.

Tevi & Tashi
  Bradford
David J Bradley
Johnny Brainwash
Laura Bramble
Pancake Oliver
  Brandt
Madeleine Bregulla
Danni and Izzy
  Brennand
Elian Bright
Molly Anne Bright
Julien Brochet
Steven Broka
Ash Brook
Mark Brown
Kara Buchanan
Erica Bullivant
Kirby Bullock
Sabine Burgard
Gem Burgess
Alex Burns
Christine Burns
Chris Butler
Kate Calico
Herta Calvo-Faugier
Riley Camps
Olivia Carlton
Tracy Carrithers
Alexander Carroll
Carrot
Harvey Carter
Charles M Casetti
Elara Caster
Alex Castledine

Laurie Caulfield
Rohan Chadwick
Chai (he/him)
Edward Chan
Heather Chappelle
Elizabeth Charlton
Robert Chipperfield
Claire
clarityat3am
Lauren Clarke
Shona Louise Cobb
Jaclyn Cohen
Rachel Coleman
Carolina Cordero
Clodagh Corry
Lou Coues
Alex Coughlan
Gayle Coulter
Danielle Cowley
Jane Crawford
Dylan Creighton
Sarah Creighton
Gemma Curtis
Dafydd
Levi Darbyshire
Kat Davenport
Bree Davidson
Theresa Davis
Donna DeFilippi
Caroline Delbert
Paige Demoe
Jamie Dempster
Joey den Broeder
River Deng
Peter Desmet

Matthew Dimitroff
Kayleigh Doherty
Michael Dominis
Mags Donaldson
Ben Doran
Bronwyn Driver
Michelle Druce
Kelli Dunham
Adam Duston
Lewis Eason
M Eck
Daniel Edmondson
Courtney
  Edmundson
Nia Edwards-Behi
Lisa Egan
Jaco Eirian
Rola El Jammal
Mitra Elgrail
Eli
Jenny Elizabeth
Elizabeth
Hayley Ellis-Williams
Sasha Elster
John Etherington
Ellis Evans
Kate Evans
Toby Fair
Maria Fallon
Hannah Fear
Katie Fenn
Madeleine Fenner
Lisa Ferreira
Colleen Flanagan
Eimear Flynn

Theresa Flynn
Lisa Foley
For my brilliant sister
    Edith
Charity Forrester
Heather Frank
Jack Freeman
Sandy Gale
Aisling Gallagher
James Gallagher
Diakhoumba
    Gassama
Jude Gates
Amro Gebreel
Geertje & Nellie
Seth Gerrits
Margaret Gilbert
Katie Giles
Carlin Gilroy
Gingercapp / KC
Bruno Girin
Stephen Glenn
Theo Glover
Basia Godel
Stephanie Goodner
Jarod Gouldie
Samantha Gowdy
Chad Gowler
Allie Grace
Caroline Grace
Charlotte Grace
James Graham
TheoJane Graham
Georgia Grainger
Nina Grant

Tim Grauwiler
Jamie Graves
Viviane Gravey
Nick Gray
Rachel Green
Brytt Greenwood
Grace Greuel
Victoria Grieve
Megan Griffin-
    Pickering
Emily Griffith
Hugh Griffiths
Katy Guest
Jessica Gunnoe
Gwen
Méabh H
Anna H.
Mary H. and Freja
    the Cat
Kristen Hadley
Morgan Hale
Lou Hales
Ben Hall
Elijah Hall
Sophie Hall
Alice Handley
Hann, Gillian
    & Tony
Eli Hanna
Fergal Hanna
Euan Hardgrave
Will Harding
William Harding
Elisabeth Harrison
Victoria Hart

Emily 'blueish'
    Hathaway
Ruth Haverty
Anna Hayhurst
Heather and Chris
Sarah Hecker
Marlies Heijkoop
Ernst Heijn
HelloLovelyScientist
Johannes Hermansson
Will Heron
Gary Herreman
Caroline Hill
Alyssa & Kris
    Hinds-Honsowetz
Sarah Hodne
Chris Hogan
Devin Hogan
Ash Sorrel Holland
Beth Hollins
Jade Howey
Jamie Edan Macleod
    Hughes
Nikolai Huiras
Abbie Hunt
James Ingham
Jesse Irwin
Hayley A. Jackson
Peter Jacobson
Kyle Jakubowska
Erin Jameson
Maike Jansen
Marta Lønne Jensen
Erin Jerison
Joe

Jasmine Johansson
Tanya Jones
Jennifer Jordan
Kyle Jordan
Daniel Joy
Neil Kaplan-Kelly
Gemma Katy
Annette Kavanaugh
Lily Kazinka
Jim Kelley
Andrew Kenney
Mary Kersey
Miles Kidson
Dan Kieran
Kelly Kietur
A Kimbell
Paige Kimble
Kira
Sev Kires
Kittenseses
Doreen Knight
Vallerie Knight
Sarah Knowles
Iida Koivunen
Arthur Krauß
Laec Krauß
Cheryl Lackman
Genevieve Lajeunesse
Alex Lanao
Holly Lawton
Rebecca Le
Cara Blu Legender
Em LeMaster
Elizabeth Liddle
Caroline Lloyd

Jenna Lockman
Melanie Love
Kelyn Lucas
Constance Lynch
Síofra Lynch
Angela Madden
Laura Magnier
Conal Maguire
Megan Maguire
Catt** Makin
Napat Malathum
Philippa Manasseh
Azrael Mandera
Kara Marang
Rebecca Martin
Wesley Mason
Cheryl Mathieu
Katie May and
    Flossie Boyd
Claire MB
Laura McAdam
Aidan McCabe
Smokey & Kelly
    McColman
Paul McConville
Kathleen McCormack
Helena McCoy
Rachel McCraw
Helen McElwee
Sean McGettrick
Katy McGilvray
Andrew McGlothlin
Luke McKeand
Maura McLaughlin
Peter McMinn

Heather McNamee
Shannon McNamee
Trotsky McNulty
Denise McSpadden
Laura McVey
Alan Meban
Melzy_rose90 (Melissa)
Mikko Merioksa
Rowan Michaels
Beth Milford-Jones
Alison Millar
Leo Miller
Jordan Milly
    Millward
Milo (transkiwi)
Chloë Minish
Shrew Mist
John Mitchinson
Asia Miyai
Cress Moberg
Isaac Mockford
Sarah Mongiat
Marion Moreau
Juliette Morfin
Jeremy Morgan
Chris Morris
Willow & Izzy &
    Jennyfurr Morris
James Morrison
Bobby Moss
MQW
Ethan Mudie
AE Mulholland
Jaffrey and Zeke
    Mullen-Cole

Autumn Murphy
Gráinne Murray
Audrey Musselman-
    Brown
Hugh N
Carlo Navato
Sally Newbrook
Honor Nicol
Mallaidh Caitlín
    Nig-Uidhir
Alexis Norman
notmoro
Nova
Harriet Oliver $
    Bowtie Novak
Phil Nulty
Cass O Sullivan
Emma O'Brien
Richard O'Keeffe
Mark O'Neill
Niamh O'Reilly
Robert O'Sullivan
Emma O'Brien
Ingrid Ockert
Kelsey Ockert
Madditt og Beta
Laura Ohman
Theodor Olaussen
Beth Oliver
Alicia Orellana
Melissa Otto
Cameron Owen
Justin Owlett
Victor Pantea
Trish Paton

Doug Paulley
Jessica Pautler
Alex Pearce
Matt Peperell
Ben Bird Person
Kat Peverelle-Lee
Megan Phillips
John Pitt
Pixie and Coco
May Plumb
Antonia Helena
    Pokorny
Justin Pollard
Sion Moisha Pope
Scott Potterie
Sunniva Holm
    Poulsen
Frey Prevett
Amanda Price
Christina Pullman
Courtney Pursell
Ryan Putnam
Queen Cynthia Cat
Robert Quinn
Rachel & Calum
Bouncy Rainbo
Joanna Ramsay-Patel
Kate Ray
Robin Rea
Cat Reilly
Rhys Renken
Andrea Reynolds
Mara Reynolds
Whitney Reynolds
Helen Rich

Hannah Ridge
Patrick Riedel
Eric Rivas
Nicole Rivette
James Roach
Anita Roberts
Fiona Robertson
Rebecca Robson
Martina Astrid Rodda
Francesca Rogers
Molly Rogers
Steve, Mackenzie,
    and Gordon
    Romenesko
Laura Roose
Kat Rose
Sean Rudenick
Gregory Ruffa
Meredith Rupp
Emily Russ
Helen Ryan
Ryl
C N Sainsbury
Alexia Salavrakos
Colin Samuel
San
Jess Sandin
Ashley Sawatzke
Em Schmitt
Brooke Schubert
Will Schultheis
Scott
Rebecca Seibel
Pamela Sentman
Jacob Sharpe

Kat Shaw
Sohaib Jubran Sheikh
Bethany Shenise
Karl Sherratt
Gillian Shorter
Jenn Siegel
Lauren Siegert
Elizabeth Siemer
Phoebe Simpson
Elin Sinclair
MLE Slone
Tor Smith
Siobhan Smyth
Snow
Caterina Soave
solaris_here / Sorin
Eden Soleilune
Pleuvonics Somers
James Spencer
Jason and Sammy
    Spriggs
Deirdre Stacey
Ross Stalker
Nick Stefan
Finlay Stevenson
Aud Ruge Stokka
Lois Stone
Kerry Strange
Meghan Strapec
Josie Stripe
Alison Sykora
Emma Sykora
Erick Taht
Nicola Tanner
Oli Taylor

Patrick Taylor
Theresa
Holly Thomas
Joelle Thomas
Alex Thomson
Indigo Thornton-
    Start
Melodious Thunk
Jennifer Tifft
TL
Tony
trashartiste/Tash
Eli Treadgold
Joe Turner
Simon Turner
Alex Turnpenny
Alexa Van Vliet
Elizabeth Veldon
Toni Velikova
Void Cat Jools
Kay Voyles
Jill Vranken
Vrolki
Alex W
Kimberly Wagner
Poppy Walters
Adam Warren
    (www.adamw.uk)
Andi, Dan, and Nate
    Watson
Max Watson
Ryan Watson
Gina Watts
Rose Weeks
Shelley Wells

Katie Weston
Michelle Westwater
Isla Whateley
Peter White
Betty Widerski
Erin Wigham
Luke Wilkes
Douglas Williams
Beth Wilson
Kirsten Wilson
Robert Wing
Zac Winter
Lauren Wisniewski
Spencer Wojtyna
David Wood
Harmony Wood
Rohan Woodcock
Maggie Woodward
Kathryn Wooldridge
SueAlex Wright
Robin Wu
Arthur Wyatt
Sara Wynn
Debbie Wythe
Kazuki Yamada
Maison Yaroch
Karen Zack
Julie Zeraschi
Lilac Zier